# REVISING KNOWLEDGE

## CLASSROOM TECHNIQUES TO HELP STUDENTS EXAMINE THEIR DEEPER UNDERSTANDING

# REVISING KNOWLEDGE

## CLASSROOM TECHNIQUES TO HELP STUDENTS EXAMINE THEIR DEEPER UNDERSTANDING

Ria A. Schmidt and Robert J. Marzano

With Laurine Halter, Tracy L. Ocasio, and Deana Senn

Learning Sciences
MARZANO
CENTER

1400 Centrepark Blvd, Suite 1000
West Palm Beach, FL 33401
717-845-6300

email: pub@learningsciences.com
learningsciences.com

Printed in the United States of America

20  19  18  17  16          1  2  3  4

Publisher's Cataloging-in-Publication Data

Halter, Laurine.
  Revising knowledge : classroom techniques to help students examine their deeper understanding / Laurine Halter [and] Robert J. Marzano.
      pages cm. – (Essentials for achieving rigor series)
   ISBN: 978-1-941112-08-3 (pbk.)
1. Effective teaching. 2. Learning, Psychology of. 3. Learning strategies. 4. Education—Aims and objectives. 5. Visual education. I. Marzano, Robert J. II. Title.
  LB1060 .H342 2015
  370.1523—dc23
                        [2014939205]

The *Essentials for Achieving Rigor* series of instructional guides helps educators become highly skilled at implementing, monitoring, and adapting instruction. Put it to practical use immediately, adopting day-to-day examples as models for application in your own classroom.

## Books in the series:

*Identifying Critical Content: Classroom Techniques to Help Students Know What Is Important*

*Examining Reasoning: Classroom Techniques to Help Students Produce and Defend Claims*

*Recording & Representing Knowledge: Classroom Techniques to Help Students Accurately Organize and Summarize Content*

*Examining Similarities & Differences: Classroom Techniques to Help Students Deepen Their Understanding*

*Processing New Information: Classroom Techniques to Help Students Engage with Content*

*Revising Knowledge: Classroom Techniques to Help Students Examine Their Deeper Understanding*

*Practicing Skills, Strategies & Processes: Classroom Techniques to Help Students Develop Proficiency*

*Engaging in Cognitively Complex Tasks: Classroom Techniques to Help Students Generate & Test Hypotheses across Disciplines*

*Creating & Using Learning Targets & Performance Scales: How Teachers Make Better Instructional Decisions*

*Organizing for Learning: Classroom Techniques to Help Students Interact within Small Groups*

# Table of Contents

Visit www.learningsciences.com/bookresources to download materials from this book.

# Acknowledgments

Learning Sciences International would like to thank the following reviewers:

Jen Haberling
2009 Michigan Teacher of the Year
Baldwin Street Middle School
Hudsonville, Michigan

Derek Olson
2009 Minnesota Teacher of the Year
Afton-Lakeland Elementary
Stillwater, Minnesota

Deb Fogg
2009 New Hampshire Teacher
    of the Year
Lancaster School
Lancaster, New Hampshire

Rebecca Snyder
2009 Pennsylvania Teacher of the
    Year
Greater Latrobe Senior High School
Latrobe, Pennsylvania

Wanda Lacy
2013 Tennessee Teacher of the Year
Farragut High School
Knoxville, Tennessee

Amy L. Weems
2013 Louisiana Teacher of the Year
Ouachita Junior High School
Monroe, Louisiana

# About the Authors

**RIA A. SCHMIDT, PhD,** is an educational professional with more than 15 years of experience as a Teacher, Principal, Central Office Administrator, and Staff Developer. Dr. Schmidt's experience in curriculum and instruction includes creating and presenting professional-development sessions for teachers and administrators on differentiation, rubrics, assessment (formative/summative), proficiency scoring, standards and benchmarks, standards-based education, and standards-based reporting; successfully guiding a school system transition from traditional grading/report cards to a standards-based reporting system; and coordinating standardized assessments and data usage in schools for the purpose of state reporting and informing instruction. In addition, Dr. Schmidt has experience in observing and evaluating both teachers and school administrators.

**ROBERT J. MARZANO, PhD,** is CEO of Marzano Research Laboratory and Executive Director of the Learning Sciences Marzano Center for Teacher and Leader Evaluation. A leading researcher in education, he is a speaker, trainer, and author of more than 150 articles on topics such as instruction, assessment, writing and implementing standards, cognition, effective leadership, and school intervention. He has authored over 30 books, including *The Art and Science of Teaching* (ASCD, 2007) and *Teacher Evaluation That Makes a Difference* (ASCD, 2013).

**LAURINE HALTER, MSEd,** has an education career that spans more than 20 years. She has the unique distinction of being awarded the South Dakota Division of Workforce and Career Preparation's Award for Special Educational Programming in Science. She earned her master's degree at South Dakota State University.

**TRACY L. OCASIO, EDd,** with more than 25 years in education, was a successful assistant superintendent and principal prior to working at Learning Sciences International.

**DEANA SENN, MSSE,** is the Lead Content Developer and a Senior Staff Developer for Learning Sciences Marzano Center. Her experience spans the United States and Canada in both rural and urban settings. Ms. Senn received her BS from Texas A&M University and MS from Montana State University.

# Introduction

This guide, *Revising Knowledge: Classroom Techniques to Help Students Examine Their Deeper Understanding,* is intended as a resource for improving a specific strategy of instructional practice: revising knowledge.

Your motivation to incorporate this strategy into your instructional toolbox may have come from a personal desire to improve your instructional practice through the implementation of a research-based set of strategies (such as those found in the Marzano instructional framework) or a desire to increase the rigor of the instructional strategies you implement in your classroom so that students meet the expectations of demanding standards such as the Common Core State Standards, Next Generation Science Standards, C3 Framework for Social Studies State Standards, or state standards based on or influenced by College and Career Readiness Anchor Standards.

This guide will help teachers of all grade levels and subjects improve their performance of a specific instructional strategy: revising knowledge. Narrowing your focus on a specific skill, such as revising knowledge, allows you to concentrate on the nuances of this instructional strategy so you can deliberately improve it. This allows you to intentionally plan, implement, monitor, adapt, and reflect on this single element of your instructional practice. A person seeking to become an expert displays distinctive behaviors, as explained by Marzano and Toth (2013):

- breaks down the specific skills required to be an expert

- focuses on improving those particular critical skill chunks (as opposed to easy tasks) during practice or day-to-day activities

- receives immediate, specific, and actionable feedback, particularly from a more experienced coach

- continually practices each critical skill at more challenging levels with the intention of mastering it, giving far less time to skills already mastered

This series of guides will support each of the previously listed behaviors, with a focus on breaking down the specific skills required to be an expert and giving day-to-day practical suggestions to enhance these skills.

# Building on the Marzano Instructional Model

This series is based on the Marzano instructional framework, which is grounded in research and provides educators with the tools they need to connect instructional practice to student achievement. The series uses key terms that are specific to the Marzano model of instruction. See Table 1, Glossary of Key Terms.

**Table 1: Glossary of Key Terms**

| Term | Definition |
|---|---|
| CCSS | Common Core State Standards is the official name of the standards documents developed by the Common Core State Standards Initiative (CCSSI), the goal of which is to prepare students in the United States for college and career. |
| CCR | College and Career Readiness Anchor Standards are broad statements that incorporate individual standards for various grade levels and specific content areas. |
| Desired result | The intended result for the student(s) due to the implementation of a specific strategy. |
| Monitoring | The act of checking for evidence of the desired result of a specific strategy while the strategy is being implemented. |
| Instructional strategy | A category of techniques used for classroom instruction that has been proven to have a high probability of enhancing student achievement. |
| Instructional technique | The method used to teach and deepen understanding of knowledge and skills. |
| Content | The knowledge and skills necessary for students to demonstrate standards. |
| Scaffolding | A purposeful progression of support that targets cognitive complexity and student autonomy to reach rigor. |
| Extending | Activities that move students who have already demonstrated the desired result to a higher level of understanding. |

The educational pendulum swings widely from decade to decade. Educators move back and forth between prescriptive checklists and step-by-step lesson plans to approaches that encourage instructional autonomy with minimal regard for the science of teaching and need for accountability. Two practices are often missing in both of these approaches to defining effective instruction: 1) specific statements of desired results, and 2) solid research-based connections. The Marzano instructional framework provides a comprehensive system that details what is required from teachers to develop their craft using research-based instructional strategies. Launching from this solid instructional foundation, teachers will then be prepared to merge that science with their own unique, yet effective, instructional style, which is the art of teaching.

*Revising Knowledge: Classroom Techniques to Help Students Examine Their Deeper Understanding* will help you grow into an innovative and highly skilled teacher who is able to implement, scaffold, and extend instruction to meet a range of student needs.

## Essentials for Achieving Rigor

This series of guides details essential classroom strategies to support the complex shifts in teaching that are necessary for an environment where academic rigor is a requirement for all students. The instructional strategies presented in this series are essential to effectively teach the CCSS, the Next Generation Science Standards, or standards designated by your school district or state. They require a deeper understanding, more effective use of strategies, and greater frequency of implementation for your students to demonstrate the knowledge and skills required by rigorous standards. This series includes instructional techniques appropriate for all grade levels and content areas. The examples contained within are grade-level specific and should serve as models and launching points for application in your own classroom.

Your skillful implementation of these strategies is essential to your students' mastery of the CCSS or other rigorous standards, no matter the grade level or subject you are teaching. Other instructional strategies covered in the Essentials for Achieving Rigor series, such as analyzing errors in reasoning and engaging students in cognitively complex tasks, exemplify the cognitive complexity needed to meet rigorous standards. Taken as a package, these strategies may at first glance seem quite daunting. For this reason, the series focuses on just one strategy in each guide.

# Revising Knowledge

Revising knowledge to help students examine their deeper understanding of critical content is an instructional strategy comprised of multiple discrete cognitive processes that includes 1) reviewing prior knowledge; 2) identifying and correcting mistakes, misconceptions, or misunderstandings; 3) identifying gaps in knowledge; 4) amending prior knowledge; and 5) explaining the underlying reasons for specific knowledge revisions. Each of these aspects of revising knowledge, when directly taught to and modeled for your students, has the potential not only to deepen their content knowledge but also enhance their memory and problem-solving abilities related to critical content.

The process of revising knowledge is not confined to classrooms or schools. Individuals at every age and stage of development are constantly revising their prior learning by correcting errors and misconceptions as well as adding new information. The difference between this almost unconscious ongoing learning process and the revising knowledge strategy is this: you, the classroom teacher, must intentionally teach and model the process for students to ensure that they acquire critical content knowledge.

There are two types of knowledge: declarative and procedural. Declarative knowledge is informational in nature, while procedural knowledge involves strategies, skills, and processes. The discipline of cognitive psychology describes the process of how individuals acquire knowledge using two terms: *schema* and *schemata*. Schema is thought to be the structure of how concepts are stored in memory, and schemata represents how those concepts are organized based on our experience and others' perspectives. There are three types of schema development, and they are directly related to revising knowledge:

- Accretion is the addition of new knowledge into existing memory.

- Tuning the schema evolves to become more consistent with experience.

- Restructuring is when new information does not fit into the current schema and results in the reorganizing or creation of new schema (Marzano, 2007).

The biggest mistake you can make in your implementation of revising knowledge is to forget whose knowledge needs to be revised. If your students are dutifully copying your notes or outlines from the board or writing down every word of your lectures, the knowledge is yours, not theirs. If your students plug into their notebooks a graphic organizer that you created, it does not represent their knowledge. It represents yours.

The big idea of revising knowledge is this: Students cannot revise or amend knowledge unless they have personally processed the information in various ways to include recording and representing their own interpretations and understandings of the content. You can only harness the power inherent in revising previous knowledge if your students own the previous knowledge.

## The Effective Implementation of Revising Knowledge

There are six steps to the effective implementation of revising knowledge:

1. Directly teach and model the five aspects of revising knowledge.

2. Become skilled in executing the six techniques for revising knowledge.

3. Create a classroom climate in which risk taking is encouraged and supported.

4. Harness the power of cooperative learning to keep all of your students engaged in revising prior understandings.

5. Continually remain focused on student mastery of critical content as the ultimate goal of your instructional efforts.

6. Gradually release responsibility to students for managing their own thinking and learning by revising their previous knowledge.

### Directly Teach and Model the Five Aspects of Revising Knowledge

There are five aspects of revising knowledge. Before students can revise their own thinking and understanding about critical content, they must understand precisely what revising their prior learning entails: 1) reviewing prior understanding of content, 2) identifying and correcting mistakes, 3) identifying gaps in knowledge and filling in these gaps, 4) deciding where to amend prior knowledge, and 5) explaining the reasons behind revising prior learning. All of these aspects require students to continually process critical content: reading, thinking, writing, drawing, solving, manipulating, and talking about their learning in large group discussions, with their partners, or with teachers. The five aspects are not necessarily sequential in nature as just enumerated, but all of them are essential to knowledge revision.

## Become Skilled in Executing the Six Techniques for Revising Knowledge

The six techniques for revising knowledge found in this guide are meant to serve as springboards from which to focus more of your students' attention on revising their prior understandings of content. At all costs, avoid feeling pressured to cover the content, test the content, and forget the content. This approach frequently results in students with misconceptions and gaps in their content knowledge. The six techniques for revising students' prior learning use the following resources and tools: 1) five basic tools, 2) academic notebooks, 3) content vocabulary notebooks, 4) visual tools, 5) writing, and 6) homework.

## Create a Supportive Classroom Climate

Revising knowledge requires a supportive, positive, and nonthreatening classroom environment. Revising knowledge takes courage and confidence. Some ways to encourage risk taking during revision are 1) share examples of how you take risks by revising your ideas and approaches using examples from your teaching experience; 2) share examples of revising your knowledge about classroom content; 3) share examples of famous individuals who tried and failed, yet continued to take risks; 4) display quotations and slogans that highlight the importance of taking risks and learning from mistakes; 5) allow students to try, gain new insights, revise, and then produce a final product; and 6) establish a collaborative atmosphere where students can receive help from peers when revising knowledge as well as listening to classmates' thinking about revising knowledge.

## Harness the Power of Cooperative Learning

Do not make the mistake of thinking that you are the only individual in the classroom who is creative and intelligent enough to think deeply about learning. Your students, even those who seem reticent and reluctant, have much to contribute. Use a variety of grouping arrangements (pairs, triads, and larger groups), as well as powerful processing activities, to motivate your students' energies to examine what they currently understand about critical content, and then revise prior learning.

## Focus on Content

No matter which of the six techniques you choose for teaching your students how to revise knowledge, remain focused on critical content. As you become more skilled in applying this strategy, you will see remarkable changes in students' abilities to process and understand content. They will be able to self-manage their thinking, draw conclusions, and refine schema independently. You can effectively implement this strategy by engaging students in the many different instructional techniques found in this guide or developing your own techniques.

## Gradually Release Responsibility for Thinking to Students

You can easily lose sight of your defining role as a teacher: *getting your students ready to assume total responsibility for revising their own knowledge.* Expecting students to copy your notes and graphic organizers from the board and dictating to students how their sentence stems should be completed are two ways to diminish your students' opportunities to learn.

As you consider how to effectively implement revising knowledge, note the following key teacher behaviors:

- directly teaching and modeling how to revise knowledge during the learning process

- using techniques that require students to make additions and deletions to previous knowledge

- providing opportunities for students to examine previously recorded knowledge

- prompting students to correct errors and misconceptions as well as add new information

- asking students how a specific lesson changed their perceptions and understandings of previous content

- providing students with opportunities to explain how their understanding has changed

- prompting students to revise their knowledge on a recurring basis as they deepen their understanding of critical content

- expecting students to revise their own knowledge without being prompted

- expecting students to seek out adaptations to their own learning when necessary

As you acquire expertise in the implementation of this strategy, think about how to avoid some of the following common mistakes:

- The teacher fails to plan for the revision of knowledge during every stage of learning.

- The teacher fails to provide opportunities for students to deepen or practice new learning before revising knowledge.

- The teacher fails to hold students accountable for revising their understanding.

- The teacher fails to monitor students for understanding information throughout the revision process.

## Failing to Plan for the Ongoing Revision of Knowledge

This strategy requires that students revise knowledge at several different stages of their learning. This includes when they are originally exposed to new information and after each additional exposure or opportunity to practice when new information has been added. At these points, you will ask students to make entries in their academic notebooks or in specific note-taking templates you require of your students. After every additional critical-input experience that builds on the initial learning, expect students to once again revisit and review their notes.

## Failing to Provide Opportunities to Deepen or Practice Knowledge in Advance of Revising Knowledge

During an effective learning sequence, students receive multiple exposures to declarative knowledge and/or multiple opportunities to practice procedural knowledge. After each of these exposures/opportunities, students should be given an opportunity to revise their prior learning based on increased understandings of the content. Without opportunities to deepen and practice knowledge in advance of revising knowledge, students will not be able to identify errors and correct them or amend their knowledge with additional information.

### Failing to Hold Students Accountable for Identifying Errors and Making Appropriate Changes

For the process of revising knowledge to achieve its desired result, students need to do the thinking, reviewing, revising, and amending. If teachers point out the errors in students' thinking and then dictate word for word the appropriate corrections or additions that are necessary, students will not receive the benefits of revising knowledge—deeper understanding and increased fluency in executing processes. Guard against thinking that your students are not capable enough to revise knowledge. They will be if you give them sufficient numbers of critical-input experiences followed by opportunities for group work, processing activities, and guided practice.

### Failing to Monitor Students for Understanding Information During Revision

Merely implementing this strategy by going through the motions is not sufficient. A highly effective implementation includes monitoring students' progress toward the desired result. This includes checking for correct understandings and revisions along the progression of learning.

The important attribute of revising knowledge is the role it plays in ensuring that students really understand information or procedures before they move on to more complex learning, applications of their learning, or more in-depth procedures.

## Monitoring for the Desired Result

Effective implementation of revising knowledge requires more than merely providing students with opportunities for revision. Effective implementation also includes monitoring. Monitoring is checking for evidence of the desired result of the strategy during implementation. In other words, effective implementation of a strategy includes monitoring for the desired result of that strategy in real time. The essential question is, did your students deepen/practice the information taught? A more specific question to be addressed is, was the desired result of the strategy achieved? The most elaborately planned lessons can be exercises in futility unless they begin with instructional strategies in mind, focus on standards, and are monitored by the teacher for the desired results.

There are multiple ways teachers can monitor whether the majority of students are achieving the desired result of revising knowledge. Here are some ways to tell if your students are deepening their understanding through making additions and deletions to previous knowledge:

- Students make corrections and/or additions to information previously recorded about content.

- Students can explain previous errors or misconceptions they had about content.

- Students demonstrate a growth mind-set by self-correcting errors as knowledge is revised.

- Students' revisions demonstrate alternative ways to execute procedures.

## Teacher Self-Reflection

As you improve your expertise in teaching students to revise prior learning, reflecting on what works and does not work can help you become more successful in the implementation of this strategy. Use the following set of reflection questions as a guide:

1. How can you begin to incorporate some aspects of this strategy into your instruction?

2. How can you use the strategy to help your students more effectively revise their prior learning?

3. How could you monitor and obtain evidence that the majority of students are able to revise knowledge?

4. How might you adapt and create new techniques for revising knowledge?

5. What are you learning about your students as you adapt and create new techniques?

# Instructional Techniques to Help Students Revise Knowledge

There are many ways to help your students deepen knowledge as they review, correct, and revise their understandings of declarative knowledge and practice and revise the various processes of procedural knowledge. Your ultimate goal for students is their mastery of grade-level or content standards. The ways you choose to plan for revision of knowledge during a specific lesson or unit will depend on your grade, the content, and your students. These various methods of revising knowledge are called instructional techniques. This guide contains descriptions of how to implement the following techniques:

- Instructional Technique 1: Revising Knowledge Using the Five Basic Tools

- Instructional Technique 2: Revising Knowledge Using Academic Notebooks

- Instructional Technique 3: Revising Knowledge Using Content Vocabulary Notebooks

- Instructional Technique 4: Revising Knowledge Using Visual Tools

- Instructional Technique 5: Revising Knowledge Using Writing Tools

- Instructional Technique 6: Revising Knowledge Using Homework Revision

All of the techniques are similarly organized and include the following components:

- a brief introduction to the technique

- ways to effectively implement the technique

- common mistakes to avoid as you implement the technique

- examples and nonexamples from elementary and secondary classrooms using selected learning targets

- ways to monitor for the desired result

- ways to scaffold and extend instruction to meet the needs of students

## Instructional Technique 1

# REVISING KNOWLEDGE USING THE FIVE BASIC TOOLS

The simplest definition of revising knowledge is *changing one's mind*. For example, you have no doubt gradually or even suddenly realized that something you once held to be an accurate statement of fact or the most efficient way of doing things does not make sense to you anymore. At that point, you likely review the facts regarding some piece of declarative knowledge you have held dear or mentally walk through a long-held routine of procedural knowledge and then get the creeping feeling that there are some problems. Soon thereafter, you begin to fill in your knowledge gaps with more accurate information, and eventually you revise your knowledge. As you continue to review your prior knowledge, you eventually create your own construction of new knowledge, and soon it finds a permanent home in the schema of your long-term memory. You are something of an expert in revising your own knowledge. Now, as a classroom teacher, you must make this almost invisible process become visible to your students. The following technique will help you to do that.

## How to Effectively Implement Revising Knowledge Using the Five Basic Tools

Recall that the five basic tools for revising knowledge are subroutines of revising knowledge: 1) reviewing prior understanding of content, 2) identifying and correcting mistakes, 3) identifying gaps in knowledge and filling in these gaps, 4) deciding where to amend prior knowledge, and 5) explaining the reasons behind revising prior learning.

There are several preparatory steps you must take before you will be ready to teach your students how to revise their prior knowledge. Figure 1.1 enumerates those steps. Once you have reviewed and taken those steps, you will be ready to implement revising knowledge using the basics. Once you have mastered the basics of revising knowledge, you can apply them using any of the remaining techniques found in this guide or any techniques you develop on your own.

**Figure 1.1: Seven Steps to Implementing the Basics of Revising Knowledge**

| Step to Implement the Basics | Explanatory Notes for the Teacher |
|---|---|
| 1. Master the definitions as well as the cognitive processes that comprise revising knowledge. | Begin to create scenarios in your mind that you could share with students as examples of how you have revised prior learning about critical content. Or, share an example from your personal life that might resonate with students. Your goal is to help them realize that this is not a mysterious process but one in which all thinking individuals engage. |
| 2. Develop a set of student-friendly definitions appropriate to the age/grade of your students. | Figure 1.2 displays two sets of student-friendly definitions: one for younger students and one for older students. Review these definitions, and revise as needed so you are comfortable and fluent in your use of them with students. Your goal is to make the vocabulary of knowledge revision used and understood on a daily basis. |
| 3. If appropriate, prepare a wall poster containing the definitions you have selected. | Figure 1.3 is an example of a simple poster for younger students. |
| 4. Directly teach the student-friendly definitions while also briefly modeling what the specific aspect looks and sounds like. | Table 1.1 is a lesson plan for how to teach and model the five aspects of revising prior learning. |
| 5. Directly teach the meanings, and model the various aspects of the process using familiar critical content. | The reason for using familiar content is to avoid the cognitive overload that can occur when students have to toggle back and forth between learning a new process and trying to understand new content. |
| 6. Decide where your students will be recording and representing the new learning that they will ultimately revise during the course of a chapter or unit of instruction. | You have several options for where your students will record or represent new knowledge, including 1) a template you have designed and copied for students to use and 2) an interactive, academic, or vocabulary notebook students have purchased. Figure 1.5 contains a revision template, and Resource: Academic Notebook Example is a sample of an interactive notebook. |
| 7. Make sure that all students have either recorded knowledge (written notes, key words and phrases, or sentences), solved problems, and/or represented knowledge (using drawings, pictographs, or graphic organizers). | This step in getting ready to teach and model the process of revising prior knowledge presupposes that your students have acquired some routines in your classroom relative to making notes or summarizing things they have learned. Figure 1.8 describes the way that students will acquire the new knowledge they record. |

Use the student-friendly definitions in Figure 1.2 to anchor the process of knowledge revision in your classroom. Being able to name, define, and discuss their thinking processes in terms of these five aspects will develop students' abilities to think more deeply about critical content.

**Figure 1.2: Student-Friendly Definitions for the Five Aspects of Revising Understanding**

| Aspect of Knowledge Revision | Younger Student-Friendly Definition | Older Student-Friendly Definition |
| --- | --- | --- |
| 1. Review/revisit prior understanding of content. | Look at the picture you drew, the problem you solved, or the sentence you wrote, and see if there is anything you want to add or change. | Go back to something you recorded (wrote) or represented (drew), and give your opinion or draw a conclusion about the accuracy and completeness of your work. |
| 2. Identify and correct mistakes. | See if you can spot any mistakes, and then fix them. | Find any errors in reasoning, factual understandings, or procedural errors and correct them. |
| 3. Identify gaps in knowledge and fill in the gaps. | Figure out if there are things that are almost right but need a few more facts or steps in a math solution to make them right. | Determine if there are any partially correct or incomplete statements in your notes or drawings and add what is missing. |
| 4. Decide where to amend prior knowledge. | Think about new things you have learned since you first worked on this topic. Make changes to your work to show what you know now. | Decide what new information or procedures you have learned. Add them to your notes, drawings, or problems. |
| 5. Explain reasons for knowledge revisions. | Tell why you made the changes. | Explain your thinking about the changes you made. |

**Figure 1.3: How to Revise Knowledge Poster**

# How to Revise Knowledge

**Review: Think about what you have written and carefully read it.**

**Correct: Find your mistakes and fix them.**

**Detect: Review the books, websites, periodicals, and other resources you have found to determine which ones will give you what you need.**

**Select: Pick out what is most important in the sources you have found.**

**Connect: Put together what you have found to answer your questions.**

The anchor chart shown in Figure 1.4 provides a helpful scaffold for students who are just beginning to revise their prior learning or for older students with language or learning difficulties.

**Figure 1.4: Sample Anchor Chart for Revising Prior Learning**

1. Look at your notes or pictures very carefully. Do they make sense? Do they seem complete?

2. If you made a mistake, fix it.

3. If you left something out, put it in now.

4. Add in the new things you learned.

5. Now, tell your partner the reasons you changed things, or write a sentence telling about your changes.

**Table 1.1: Lesson Plan for Teaching and Modeling the Basics of Revising Prior Learning**

| Lesson Objective | Students will be able to understand the five basic steps for revising prior learning. |
|---|---|
| Materials Needed for the Lesson | A poster similar to the one in Figure 1.3 containing student-friendly definitions of the five aspects of revising knowledge and an example of recorded prior learning using familiar content that contains mistakes and gaps. |
| Lesson Step 1 | The teacher explains the meaning of review/revisit prior learning. The teacher displays a copy of the worksheet containing an example of prior learning. He then thinks aloud about what it means to review/revisit. He whisper reads the prior knowledge and thinks about what he wrote. He thinks aloud about some things he might want to change. |
| Lesson Step 2 | That brings the teacher to the second aspect of revising knowledge: identify and correct mistakes. He asks the students if they can spot any mistakes and tell him how to fix them. |
| | Since the content is previously learned content, students are quickly able to point out mistakes and correct them. |
| Lesson Step 3 | He goes on to give the meaning of the third aspect: identify gaps in knowledge and fill the gaps. He asks a student to come to the board and write down some things that he left out. |
| Lesson Step 4 | He then gives the meaning of the fourth aspect: Think about new things you have learned since you first worked on this topic. Make changes to this work to show what you now know. |
| Lesson Step 5 | The teacher now engages the class to explain their reasons for revising this knowledge. He adds any additional reasons that may have been uniquely his own. |

**Figure 1.5: Revision Template**

| Used to Think | Now I Know |
|---|---|
| List of some initial understandings. | How those understandings in the left-hand column changed—additional knowledge or a misunderstanding that was corrected. |

**Figure 1.6: Sample Interactive Notebook Page**

## Patrick's Interactive Notebook

| Notes | Revisions |
|---|---|
| New understandings, insights, corrections of misunderstandings, etc. | Recording/representing critical information learned through teacher presentation, processing with others, elaborating activities, etc. |

**Potential sentence starters for revision work:**

I learned that . . .

Something I have learned is . . .

I noticed that . . .

I changed my thinking about this concept when . . .

I still don't understand . . .

I used to think . . . but now I think . . .

Figure 1.7 enumerates the learning activities that must precede students' recording and representing new knowledge in a revision template or interactive notebook. Recall from the introduction that to revise knowledge, students must have some prior knowledge in terms of facts, ideas, concepts, or procedures. The following sequence is meant to be illustrative, not definitive. The content and your students dictate the time span of the various parts of the sequence.

**Figure 1.7: Sequence of Learning Activities**

| Day | Learning Activity Sequence |
|---|---|
| Part 1 | The teacher begins a new unit of content with a preview activity and follows that with an initial presentation of a critical content chunk. |
| Part 2 | The teacher stops after a "chunk" to give students a task to do with a partner or group to **P**rocess/**E**laborate on and **R**ecord/Represent their understanding of the new content. Ideally, teachers will engage students in PER between each new chunk of information. |
| Part 3 | Repeat the above cycle until all of the critical chunks of content for a lesson or unit are introduced. |
| Part 4 | Have students review the critical content chunks they learned in the previous lesson. Then, assign a "content activity" to help students deepen their understanding and/or practice skills, strategies, or processes. These activities are often more challenging and ongoing projects during which the teacher gradually releases control of learning to students. Purposeful homework may be assigned if appropriate. |
| Part 5 | Only after students have had adequate time to practice what they learned or deepened their understanding should they be expected to revise their knowledge. |

## Common Mistakes

The implementation of a new technique can often result in unanticipated mistakes. However, knowing ahead of time where problems might arise will increase your likelihood of success in implementing this technique. Watch out for these common mistakes when you teach students how to revise their prior learning using the basics:

- The teacher fails to take the time needed to plan and implement the various learning activities that are prerequisites to revising knowledge.

- The teacher fails to directly teach and model critical academic vocabulary needed by students to work with and talk about revising knowledge with peers and the teacher.

- The teacher fails to release responsibility to students for revising their own knowledge and spoon feeds too much content to students via lecture.

## Examples and Nonexamples of Revising Knowledge Using the Basic Tools

The following examples and nonexamples demonstrate revising prior learning using the five basic tools of knowledge revision in both elementary and secondary classrooms.

### Elementary Example of Revising Knowledge Using the Five Basic Tools

The learning target being addressed in this example is to *demonstrate understanding of word relationships and nuances in word meanings* (CCSS. ELA-Literacy.L2.4.E). The second-grade teacher wants her students to understand each of the aspects of revising knowledge more deeply so they can begin to assume more responsibility for executing the process. They have just completed a science unit, and although students seemed to understand the content and were able to make notes on their interactive notebook pages, revising their prior learning did not go smoothly. Students were hurried and careless about making revisions, and many students did not really seem to understand what they were supposed to be doing.

Today, the teacher plans to directly teach and model the process for her students with emphasis on the relationships between the words in the process and the particular nuances of each of the words in the context of revising prior learning. She decides to further simplify the five steps for her second-grade students and has prepared picture cues to reinforce the meanings of the words and phrases she will teach: 1) *review*, 2) *correct mistakes*, 3) *fill gaps*, 4) *add more*, and 5) *explain*.

Boys and girls, this morning we're going to learn how to do a better job of writing in our academic notebooks about things we've learned. I am going to show you how I would improve the notes that I took in my notebook so that you can improve your notes. First we're going to review. Let me show you how I review notes I've taken. I first whisper read them so that I'm sure I don't miss anything important. I am thinking while I am whisper reading that I could do a better job of writing my notes now that I've learned some new things during the week. As you review my notes, are there some things you see that I should change? *Several students point out mistakes in the teacher's notes.* I agree with you. So, after I review my notes [teacher points to the word and the picture cue], the next thing I do is correct my mistakes. I'm going to cross out some words I wrote and write in better words.

So, first, I reviewed. Then I corrected my mistakes. Now I'm going to fill my gaps. Filling in gaps means that you wrote something that was only partly correct, and you need to figure out what to write to make it completely correct. *Students point out where the teacher didn't write everything she should have to show her learning.* Now, let's go through the steps we've taken so far: we reviewed, we corrected mistakes, and we filled in the gaps with some things we forgot to write down before. Now it's time to add more. That means figuring out something brand new we learned that we didn't write in our notes. Who can give me an example of some new learning I should add to my notebook? *Students offer a number of appropriate suggestions, and the teacher writes them in her notes.*

You've done great work, class. Now, the last thing I have to do is explain. That means I have to tell you the reasons why I made the changes I did. I just can't go speeding through this without thinking about why I made the changes and added the new information that I did.

Once the teacher explains her reasons for each of the changes she made in her notes, she reviews the five new terms she has taught and modeled for students and reminds them that the five words have to work together when they are revising their prior learning. She then asks students to retrieve their academic notebooks and take a few minutes to carefully go through each of the steps in the last set of notes they took and correct mistakes, fill gaps, and add new information. Once students complete that exercise, she directs them to get together with their assigned partner and exchange notebooks. She explains that they need to figure out where their partner corrected mistakes, filled in the gaps, and added new learning. Finally, she tells them to explain to their partners why they made the changes they did. During this time, she walks around the classroom, looking over shoulders at academic notebooks, reading what students have written, and listening to their reasons for making the changes.

*Elementary Nonexample of Revising Knowledge Using the Basics*
The nonexample elementary teacher is using the same learning target and has noticed the same problems with how students are revising their prior learning and understandings of critical content. He decides to spend some time explaining the five aspects he wants students to execute. He is pressed for time and decides to skip making a poster since this is the second time that he has talked about this process with students. He is reluctant to model for his students, feeling very uncomfortable about showing them something he has written that contains mistakes, gaps, and downright omissions of critical content. So, he basically reiterates all of the information he told them when they last revised prior learning in their academic notebooks. Failing to provide visual cues and modeling to support his instruction is a big mistake. The majority of students are confused about exactly how to implement the revision of prior learning.

*Secondary Example of Revising Knowledge Using the Basics*
A high school science teacher is concerned about his students' casual and even careless approaches to revising prior learning in their interactive notebooks. The learning target for this unit is *use a model to illustrate how photosynthesis transforms light energy into stored chemical energy. Examples of models could include diagrams, chemical equations, and conceptual models* (Next Generation Science Standards, HS-LS1-5). He creates

an interactive template for students to use as they execute the basics of revising prior knowledge. See Figure 1.8, Interactive Template for Revising Prior Learning.

**Figure 1.8: Interactive Template for Revising Prior Learning**

| Read the Directions | Answer This Question | Then, Answer This Question |
|---|---|---|
| Go back to something you recorded (wrote) or represented (drew), and give your opinion or draw a conclusion about the accuracy and completeness of your work. | What is your conclusion about the accuracy and completeness of your work? | What is your reason for making this conclusion? |
| Pick out errors in reasoning or factual or procedural errors and correct them. | What errors in reasoning did you make?<br><br>What factual errors did you make? | Describe how you will correct the errors in reasoning.<br><br>Describe how you will correct the factual errors. |
| Determine if there are any partially correct or incomplete statements in your notes or drawings and add what is missing. | Where have you made incomplete statements or partial representations of the process in your notes and drawings? | Describe what you will do to fill in those gaps. |
| Decide what new information or procedures you have learned. Add them to your notes, drawings, or problems. | What new and critical information did you neglect to add to your statement of prior learning? | Describe what you are going to add. |
| Explain your thinking about the changes you made. | What will you do to avoid that in the future? | Explain your reasons for having so many errors, gaps, and omissions. |

The teacher reviews the basic steps for revising and displays a set of notes that she took based on the content—input, processing, elaboration, and recording and representing. She then walks through her notes and drawings, modeling the revision process for her students.

Class, I see that some of you are feeling a bit embarrassed at your somewhat careless approach to thinking. This particular activity is an important one for learning the content in this course.

This activity builds your deeper understanding of the various scientific processes we will learn about.

If not revised, the errors in thinking and understanding that are recorded and represented in your notebooks will bounce around in your brain during the whole semester and follow you through high school and college or your career.

*Secondary Nonexample of Revising Knowledge Using the Basics*

The nonexample teacher plans a similar lesson, but instead of developing an interactive template and modeling her own thinking about the process of revising prior learning for students, she lectures students about their deficiencies. Absent any clear guidelines, such as the interactive template and a model provided by the teacher, the students continue to work on revising their prior knowledge without making many substantive improvements.

## Determining If Students Can Revise Knowledge Using the Basics

Monitoring is comprised of two components: 1) something that students do to demonstrate the desired result of the technique—in this instance, revising their prior learning in an appropriate template or notebook, and 2) something that the teacher does to check for the desired result and respond to students' progress. Here are some specific examples of monitoring students' ability to revise prior learning:

- Students check their revisions and make needed corrections and additions. Meanwhile, the teacher moves around the room and looks at their work.

- Students turn in their written revisions, and the teacher checks to determine accuracy and clarity in their work.

- The teacher listens in on discussions partners have regarding the reasons behind the changes they have made.

The student proficiency scale in Table 1.2 shows the range of student proficiencies for how successfully students can revise prior learning to deepen and extend their critical content knowledge. Use the scale to determine the precise ways you can identify the desired result in your students.

**Table 1.2: Student Proficiency Scale for Revising Knowledge Using the Basics**

| Emerging | Fundamental | Desired Result |
|---|---|---|
| Students struggle with revising information they have recorded in the required template or notebook.<br><br>Students are unable to decide what information is needed to add or edit. | Students can identify statements that were initially correct and/or incorrect.<br><br>Students can review and add to their previous correct statements of knowledge and correct misconceptions and mistakes from previous entries.<br><br>Students are not always able to provide the reasons behind their revision decisions. | Students can successfully revise information they have recorded or represented in a template or academic notebook, providing reasons for their revisions. |

## Instructional Technique 2

# REVISING KNOWLEDGE USING ACADEMIC NOTEBOOKS

If you have not previously used academic notebooks in your classroom, first consider these guidelines:

- Academic notebooks are not a place for students to take and keep notes during teacher presentations of lessons.

- Academic notebooks are not a place to store handouts and worksheets provided by the teacher.

- Academic notebooks are not assignment notebooks containing the syllabus and a calendar of assignment due dates.

- Academic notebooks are not a repository for homework assignments.

- Academic notebooks rarely, if ever, go home with students.

So, what are academic notebooks? Academic notebooks—or, as they are often called, interactive notebooks—contain a permanent record of students' analyses and syntheses of the content they have learned. In an academic notebook, students date their entries, which include generated notes written after a short time of content input (teacher presentation, video, student reading), reactions to content, questions and answers, reflections about their progress, and revisions made throughout their learning. They might also include notes about things they want to know or questions about that day's learning experience. Academic notebooks contain a sequential record of students' understanding of the content. Perhaps you have kept artifacts of your own academic pursuits such as reports from elementary school, term papers from high school, and theses from graduate school. These written documents contain a sequential record of your growth in both declarative knowledge about various subjects and procedural knowledge as applied to the process of writing. If you have paged through these prior assignments, you may have been surprised by how little you really knew and how many mistakes you made. Perhaps they were an encouragement to you relative to your students' progress. Academic notebooks provide both the teacher and student a very visible and permanent record of their learning.

There are several organizational/scheduling/formatting issues that must be agreed upon in advance by teachers and students and then implemented with fidelity:

- As mentioned, with very few exceptions, academic notebooks will be housed in the classroom and not taken home.

- The teacher will give opportunities to students for the work of revising knowledge after each learning sequence, whether it is at the beginning of new learning or when students are deepening or practicing critical content.

- Notebooks must be formatted in such a way that space is allowed between notes and visual tools that were originally taken to record additions or cross out incorrect information.

- The ongoing process of content input from the teacher or a media presentation followed by time for processing and practice followed by recording new knowledge in the notebook should become a classroom routine.

- Notebooks can be used to consolidate learning and study in advance of a test.

## How to Effectively Revise Knowledge Using Academic Notebooks

There are several ways to teach and show your students how to revise their knowledge using academic notebooks. The first way is a prerequisite for every technique in this guide: *directly teach, model, and facilitate guided practice in revising knowledge in their academic notebooks.* Once students have become accustomed to the process of independently revising knowledge, guide them toward assuming more responsibility for this process by facilitating student-led conferences during which students are expected to reflect on their progress and ask questions about critical content. As students gain confidence in revising prior knowledge, you can also harness the power of cooperative learning by facilitating three different peer-review processes: 1) peer review and feedback, 2) consult/compare/explain, and 3) agree/disagree/explain.

## Directly Teach Students How to Revise Prior Knowledge Using Academic Notebooks

For students to revise knowledge in their academic notebooks, they will need to have recorded (written notes or made a quick outline) and/or represented (made a quick drawing or created a graphic organizer) based on the lesson sequence shown in Figure 1.7. At that point, students are ready to make entries in their academic notebook, which they do. On the following day, the teacher might show a video about the critical content and give students a few minutes to share with a partner about what they learned from this second critical-input experience that clarifies or adds to learning from the teacher's previous presentation. Now it is time to revise knowledge.

Figure 2.1 is an example lesson plan of knowledge revision based on the concept of photosynthesis. Column 1 lists the aspect of knowledge revision. Column 2 summarizes the teacher's directions to the students. Column 3 guides you through the various aspects of knowledge revision, showing you what the process looks like in an actual student's academic notebook.

You may need to review vocabulary and model the process several more times, but this investment will soon pay dividends as students begin to assume more of the responsibility for revising their prior understandings of critical content.

**Figure 2.1: Lesson Plan for Modeling Revision of Knowledge**

| Aspect of Knowledge Revision | Teacher Directions to Students | Examples From Figures 2.2 and 2.3 |
|---|---|---|
| 1. Review/revisit prior knowledge. | Read over and think about the statements you previously wrote after the teacher's presentation about photosynthesis. | Figure 2.2 is an example of a page from a student's academic notebook. The notes on the left side of the figure were written after a lesson sequence similar to the one described in Figure 1.7. |
| 2. Identify and correct mistakes. | See if you can identify any mistakes in your notes now that you have watched the video. | The right-hand column of Figure 2.2 contains the revisions the student made after identifying and correcting mistakes. Statement A indicates the mistake and correction for Statement 1 in the Notes. |
| 3. Identify gaps in knowledge. | See if there are any partially correct or incomplete statements in your notes. | Statements B and C illustrate the student identifying gaps in knowledge and restating a more accurate understanding of the process of photosynthesis. |
| 4. Amend prior knowledge. | Add some additional information to your notebook by representing your knowledge with a graphic organizer. | Statement D illustrates the student amending knowledge by creating a graphic organizer shown in Figure 2.3. |
| 5. Explain reasons for knowledge revisions. | State the reasons that you made the revisions to your knowledge. | Statement E illustrates why the student made the revisions. |

Figure 2.2 illustrates an example of revisions one student made in his academic notebook after identifying and correcting mistakes.

**Figure 2.2: Example of the Five Aspects of Revising Knowledge**

| Notes | Revisions |
|---|---|
| 1. Photosynthesis is when chlorophyll makes the leaves green. | A. I used to think that chlorophyll was one of the products of photosynthesis. This statement (#1) is wrong. Plants use chlorophyll, the stuff that makes the leaves green, to absorb the light from the sun. |
| 2. Photosynthesis is when plants absorb water through their roots. | B. I changed my thinking about the concept of photosynthesis when I watched the video. Although plants do absorb water through their roots as part of the process, that's not the whole process. Statement #2 is incomplete. I have a new idea about photosynthesis now: Photosynthesis is how plants make their own food. |
| 3. Carbon dioxide and oxygen are part of the process of photosynthesis. | C. I realize that Statement #3 is very confusing. Here's a better way to say it: Water and carbon dioxide go together and are sort of the raw materials of photosynthesis. Oxygen and glucose are what's made during the process of photosynthesis. |
| | D. I'm going to sketch this process to make sure I have everything working together the way it does during the process of photosynthesis. (See Figure 2.3 for the organizer that summarized the process for the student.) |
| | E. I made the revisions because I now have a better understanding of photosynthesis. Photosynthesis is the process through which plants make their own food. |

Information about photosynthesis adapted from Photosynthesis Video. TV411 Tune in to Learning. Education Development Center, Inc.

Figure 2.3 is a summarizer created by the student to represent his current understanding of the process of photosynthesis. As the class begins to acquire deeper learnings, the student will revise his summarizer to include additional information.

**Figure 2.3: Summarizer Illustrating the Process of Photosynthesis**

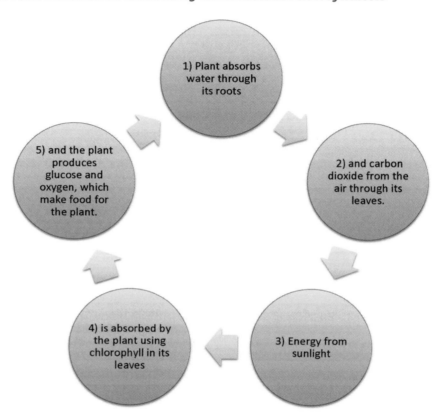

Although you will regularly monitor students' notebook entries and give periodic feedback, the following activity requires that students assume more responsibility for monitoring their own work.

## Revising Knowledge in Academic Notebooks Using a Student-Led Conference

One way to review and revise knowledge using academic notebooks takes place in the context of a student-led conference with the teacher. Individual conferences can be scheduled as requested, either by you or the student at any time, but insist that students assume responsibility for leading their conferences. One way to help students overcome their anxiety about such conferences is to role-play a conference with one or two more confident student volunteers. Regularly scheduled conferences for all students can be held on a staggered schedule over a several-day or -week period. The most productive time for these conferences is prior to and in preparation for major assessments of any kind. Here are some guidelines to make the conferences that students lead more productive:

- Require that students carefully review their notebooks in advance of the conference, jotting down any areas of confusion or framing specific questions about the content.

- Expect students to lead the conversation, but provide guidance as needed.

- Plan the conference in advance by making notes about the student to include any challenges and strengths you have identified to make the conference as productive as possible.

- Be patient with students and use wait time wisely.

- Utilize any teachable moments.

- Keep the conference to about ten to twelve minutes.

- End the conference with some follow-up suggestions for students based on your feedback and any input students have suggested.

As your students acquire the basics of revising knowledge in their academic notebooks and can engage in a productive conference with you that they lead, consider shifting even more responsibility on to students for their knowledge revision by using peer-review techniques.

## Revising Knowledge in Academic Notebooks Using Peer Review

A powerful technique for revising knowledge in academic notebooks is the use of one-to-one peer review in which students use a set of questions to guide them in reviewing each other's academic notebooks. Figure 2.4 contains a completed peer-review form based on the contents of the academic notebook entry on photosynthesis illustrated earlier in Figures 2.2 and 2.3.

Before you engage your class in this peer-review activity, model how the process should look. Once students have seen an exemplar, they will have a better idea of how to interact with their partners. Here are the directions:

1) Give each student a copy of the peer-review form. A template can be found in Resource: Template for Peer Review of an Academic Notebook. 2) Direct students to turn to their assigned partners and trade academic notebooks. 3) Ask students to quietly review the academic notebooks of their partners and quickly write answers to the questions on the form. 4) Once students have answered the questions, direct them to exchange forms and use the information shared by their peers to make any needed revisions to their notebooks.

The first time you demonstrate this activity for students, allocate more time. However, once it becomes a regular classroom routine, students should spend no more than ten minutes.

**Figure 2.4: Completed Peer-Review Form**

| Read the Question and Review Your Classmate's Academic Notebook to Decide on an Answer | Write Your Answer in This Column |
| --- | --- |
| What methods did your classmate use to represent information that was especially clear, concise, and appropriate for the information being recorded (e.g., graphic organizers, flowcharts, concept maps, drawings, or pictographs)? | *I thought the organizer with the cycle of photosynthesis was pretty good.* |
| What information did your classmate record that you did not record in your academic notebook? | *The summary statements that he wrote were very clear and easy to understand. I didn't write anything that was nearly as good.* |
| What do you think is the most important information recorded in your classmate's academic notebook? | *I think the statements are the most important information in his notebook.* |
| What is one thing that your classmate could improve on in recording knowledge in his academic notebooks? | *I think he could have done a drawing of a tree or a plant showing all the different subprocesses that are part of photosynthesis. The organizer was OK, but I would have liked a picture of a plant or tree with the different parts labeled.* |

The questions in the form are adapted from Marzano (2012). The answers are original to this guide.

## Revising Knowledge in Academic Notebooks Using Consult, Compare, and Explain

Another method for revising knowledge in academic notebooks through peer review is known as *Consult, Compare, and Explain.* In this activity, students read a peer's academic notebook, compare the peer's entries to their own, and then make revisions in their own notebooks based on their sharing. Students learn different ways to take notes, gain new perspectives on the concept, and articulate new questions they may have after the activity. Figure 2.5 is a Consult/Compare/Explain Form. A template is located in Resource: Consult/Compare/Explain Form.

**Figure 2.5: Consult/Compare/Explain Form**

| Consult: Read My Classmate's Notebook | Compare: Revise My Notebook With New Information | Explain: Share Information With My Classmate to Identify Gaps or Incorrect Information |
|---|---|---|
| 1. | | |
| 2. | | |
| 3. | | |

Peer consulting is a powerful form of cooperative learning as students have opportunities to see how classmates are recording, representing, and revising their knowledge. Collect the forms after the exercise as one way to monitor your students' progress toward the desired result of this technique: students can successfully revise information in their academic notebooks and make extensions and applications to learning using their notebooks.

## Revising Knowledge in Academic Notebooks Using Agree/Disagree/Question

A third method for revising knowledge using academic notebooks works best in a small group of between three and five members. Figure 2.6 displays the form students use to keep track of their discussions. The group members compare entries in their notebooks to a recent cycle that included teacher input, processing with a partner, and recording and representing the new knowledge in the notebook. Members of each group identify what they agree on as a group, what they disagree on, and questions they still have about the content. Groups report out to the whole class, and the teacher addresses common agreements, disagreements, and questions. Resource: Agree/Disagree/Question Form contains a blank template for use in your classroom.

**Figure 2.6: Agree/Disagree/Question Form**

| What Does Our Group Agree About? | What Does Our Group Disagree About? | What Does Our Group Still Have Questions About? |
|---|---|---|
| 1. | | |
| 2. | | |
| 3. | | |
| 4. | | |

Adapted from Marzano (2007).

## Common Mistakes

As with all instructional techniques, there are more and less effective ways to use this technique of revision using academic notebooks. Being aware of the common mistakes in advance of planning your lessons will help you create successful experiences for your students. Here are several of the common mistakes you might inadvertently make when teaching your students how to revise knowledge using their academic notebooks:

- The teacher fails to plan for revision of knowledge at every stage of the learning. Knowledge revision is not a one-time activity done at the end of a chapter or unit. It is a fluid process that occurs over and over again during the instructional cycle.

- The teacher fails to understand that neatness, accurate grammar usage, and perfect spelling are not essential for recording and representing knowledge. The goal of revising knowledge is for students to deepen their knowledge through identifying errors (both factual and reasoning) and correcting them as well as adding additional information to make an entry more accurate and complete.

- The teacher fails to model revising strategies for students. Modeling can be a think-aloud for students about how you would review and amend prior knowledge. Or, you could provide exemplars of academic notebooks for students to peruse.

- The teacher fails to take the time needed for multiple opportunities to review their prior knowledge and revise or amend it.

- The teacher fails to create an environment in which revision is thought of as a powerful and important part of the learning process.

- The teacher fails to establish and then consistently implement procedures for managing academic notebooks to include allocated space for their storage as well as allocated times and routines for revising knowledge in the notebooks.

- The teacher fails to provide students with the benefits of retention and deepening understandings of critical content by regulating and dictating to students what should or should not be included in their academic notebooks.

- The teacher fails to schedule opportunities for students to correct and amend knowledge in their notebooks in advance of summative assessments.

## Examples and Nonexamples of Revising Knowledge Using Academic Notebooks in the Classroom

Following are two examples (one elementary and one secondary) and their corresponding nonexamples of knowledge revision using academic notebooks. While reading these examples, keep in mind the common mistake noted earlier. Also, consider how a teacher might monitor for the desired result of revising knowledge in each example.

### Elementary Example of Revising Knowledge Using Academic Notebooks

The specific learning target addressed in this example is *with prompting and support, identify the main topic and retell key details of a text* (CCSS. ELA-Literacy.RI.K.2). The kindergarten teacher is using an ELA CCSS text exemplar for K–1: Clyde Robert Bulla's *A Tree Is a Plant* with illustrations by Stacey Schuett (New York: HarperCollins, 2001).

Good morning! Yesterday we read the book *A Tree Is a Plant,* and we learned a lot of facts about trees. I am going to read the book to you again today, and I would like you to listen carefully for the details the author uses to describe a tree. Remember that a detail is a fact. Every time there is a new detail, I am going to stop and ask you to draw a small picture that you think represents that detail. You can use your academic notebook for your pictures. When we are finished, you will hand in your notebooks.

*The following week, the teacher hands back the academic notebooks to the students and begins her lesson.* Remember the book we read last week, *A Tree Is a Plant*? When I read the book, I asked you to draw pictures of the important details about a tree that you heard in the book. Today, you are going to work with your partner and retell the story using the pictures you drew in your academic notebooks. After each of you has had a turn to retell the story, I would like you to use what you learned from your partner to add more details to your pictures.

*Elementary Nonexample of Revising Knowledge Using Academic Notebooks*

The elementary nonexample teacher uses the same standard and text exemplar with his kindergarten students. He has students draw pictures in their academic notebooks of the important details they learn about trees. Several days later, the students are shown a video about the characteristics of trees. The teacher does not have them go back to their academic notebooks to revise their picture notes from the week before based on the learning from the video. Opportunities for learning diminish if students do not revise knowledge after each deepening and/or practicing activity.

*Secondary Example of Revising Knowledge*
*Using Academic Notebooks*

The learning target in this secondary example is *explain the influence and ideas of the Declaration of Independence* (US History I.3, Massachusetts History and Social Science Curriculum Framework). Ninth-grade students have been studying the Declaration of Independence and the events that led to this declaration. The teacher has provided a number of opportunities to record and represent their understanding of the Declaration of Independence. After another deepening activity in which the students worked in groups to annotate the document, the teacher asks students to get their academic notebooks and revise the notes they have taken to date. Then she asks them to work in pairs and review their partner's academic notebook using a set of questions she gives them. Since this is nearing the end of the unit and she has a culminating activity that will require them to have a firm understanding of the topic, she has them participate in one more revision activity.

> Class, you did a great job working with your partners, and now we are going create a revision template on one of the blank pages in your notebooks. To create your revision template, draw a line down the middle of the page. On the left side of that page in your notebooks, please write the phrase "Used to Think," and on the right side, write the phrase "Now I Know." Write down your new/revised understanding in the right column and your previous understandings in the left. Share these with your partner.

Students work with their partners and compare their new understandings. After giving them enough time to share with their partners, she asks for volunteers to share their understandings with the whole group so everyone can benefit from the learning that happened between peers. Figure 2.7 displays a sample revision template created by one pair of students. Figure 1.5 is a blank version of this same template.

**Figure 2.7: Sample Revision Template**

| Used to Think | Now I Know |
|---|---|
| List of some initial understandings.<br><br>*I thought that the Declaration of Independence was just a political document written by politicians.* | How those understandings in the left-hand column changed—additional knowledge or a misunderstanding that was corrected.<br><br>*Now I know that it was a document written by our Founding Fathers as a demand to break ties with the British and their laws.* |

*Secondary Nonexample of Revising Knowledge*
*Using Academic Notebooks*

Our secondary nonexample is focused on the same learning target: the Declaration of Independence. A ninth-grade class is studying the Declaration of Independence and the events that led to this declaration. In this nonexample, however, the teacher moves right into the culminating activity that requires them to use the knowledge they gained since the beginning of the unit to complete a problem-solving task. Assigning such a task is not a mistake, per se. The teacher's mistake is moving forward with the problem-solving task without knowing if the notes students have recorded in their notebooks taken are accurate or comprehensive enough to help them complete the problem-solving task successfully.

## Determining If Students Can Revise Knowledge Using Academic Notebooks

As noted earlier, monitoring for a specific desired result is a critical part of effectively implementing an instructional strategy. Remember that the desired result of revising knowledge is that students can make additions and deletions to previous learning to deepen their understandings. There are a number of ways to monitor the revision of knowledge using academic notebooks. Some methods include the following:

- Students write one challenging, thought-provoking question that shows they understand the information in their notes and want to know more.

- Students review previous entries and record their revised knowledge. The teacher walks around and reads to ensure students are recording correct information and collects the notebooks to check that the entries are correct.

- Students work with partners to discuss how their knowledge has changed since they made previous entries while the teacher walks around and listens in on the conversations.

- After students revise knowledge in their academic notebooks, they close their notebooks and write one important piece of critical information on individual whiteboards or a revision card and then hold it up. This activity requires students to hold on to the information from their revisions long enough to affix it into their memories.

- Students complete an exit slip that answers a statement, such as "I used to think _____ about this topic, but now I understand _____."

Use the student proficiency scale for revising knowledge using academic notebooks shown in Table 2.1 to determine how your students are progressing in their ability to make additions and deletions to previous knowledge that deepen their understanding.

**Table 2.1: Student Proficiency Scale for Revising Knowledge Using Academic Notebooks**

| Emerging | Fundamental | Desired Result |
|---|---|---|
| Students struggle to revise notes accurately in their notebooks.<br><br>Students may be unable to decide which information needs to edited or added. | Students can identify statements that were initially correct and/or incorrect.<br><br>Students can review and add to their previous correct statements of knowledge and correct misconceptions and mistakes from previous entries. | Students can successfully revise information in their academic notebooks and also extend and apply this information to further learning. |

# Scaffold and Extend Instruction to Meet Students' Needs

As you become more skilled at helping students revise knowledge using their academic notebooks, you will find that you can more readily identify various individuals or small groups of students that need something more, or different, from your original instruction. Some students need support or scaffolding that takes them from where they are to where they need to be. You may need to challenge other students by extending the ways in which you expect them to revise knowledge. The following suggestions are meant to be illustrative. Use them to zero in on the precise needs of your students.

## Scaffolding

When you identify individuals or a small group of students who do not seem able to grasp the concept of revising knowledge, try one of the following ways to adjust your instruction:

- Determine if students need to receive more support during the period of recording and representing of their learning following critical-input experiences.

- Meet with students to go over their academic notebooks, and talk through the critical information to help students identify and correct misconceptions or to add important information.

- Provide correct information specific to each entry that you want the students to review and revise.

- Provide peer support in the form of a helpful student who can assist the struggling students in recording and representing knowledge.

## Extending

- Ask students to create questions that will show they can make connections to other material or deeper learnings that will extend their knowledge.

- Ask students to reword their entries for a specific audience—for example, a much younger student or a post on Facebook or Twitter.

- Ask students to develop a set of questions their classmates might use to help them more effectively review and revise their notebook entries.

## Instructional Technique 3

# REVISING KNOWLEDGE USING CONTENT VOCABULARY NOTEBOOKS

For many students, the biggest obstacle to acquiring critical content knowledge is lack of word knowledge. In its narrowest sense, word knowledge means knowing the meanings of lots of words. In the broadest sense, however, word knowledge means knowing about all of the linguistic facets of a word (Nagy & Scott, 1990). Acquiring word knowledge requires more than adding lots of rote definitions to one's long-term memory. Deep word knowledge emerges only when students integrate academic and content vocabulary with prior knowledge to create more complex schema. Revising prior learning is very difficult for students unless they have the right words to describe both their knowledge and thinking. Students need both definitional and contextual information about a word to comprehend it during reading and use it appropriately in class discussions and writing. Definitional information includes teaching antonyms and synonyms for new words, rewriting or restating definitions in students' own words, providing examples and nonexamples of the words, and comparing and contrasting the words and related words. Contextual information includes giving students several sentences that illustrate the word being used in different contexts, creating a short story or scenario in which the word plays a role, acting out the word or drawing a picture for younger students, asking students to create their own sentences containing the word, and using more than one new word in a sentence to help students see the relationship between words. This technique focuses on showing students how to revise prior learning using content vocabulary notebooks (McEwan, 2009).

# How to Effectively Implement Revising Knowledge Using Content Vocabulary Notebooks

Content vocabulary notebooks are similar to academic notebooks in terms of their usage, organization, and structure. They differ, however, in that they focus solely on vocabulary usage in the context of critical content. You can use content vocabulary notebooks with any content or grade level, but they are especially appropriate for younger students or older students who struggle with reading, writing, and English vocabulary or are not necessarily ready for the demands of academic notebooks.

Content vocabulary notebooks provide opportunities for students to continually revise and enlarge their prior understandings of key terms. This kind of knowledge revision increases the likelihood that students will understand and be able to access content vocabulary during critical content input. Students need as many as a dozen exposures of a term in various contexts before they can readily determine a word's meaning in the context of reading or use it correctly in their discussions and writing. Figure 3.1 displays a dozen ways to process and experience new understandings of critical content vocabulary. These various exposures to a central concept provide opportunities for students to enlarge their understanding of the content. This list is meant to be illustrative, not definitive, and these processing activities are an essential prerequisite to revising prior knowledge of content terms.

**Figure 3.1: Ways to Process, Elaborate, Record, Represent, and Practice Content Vocabulary**

| Ways for Students to Process, Elaborate, and Practice Critical Content Vocabulary | Explanatory Notes for Teacher |
|---|---|
| 1. See the word on a word wall or in a pocket chart. | Whenever you use new terms while presenting new content or in other contexts, point to the word so that students can make an association between the written word and spoken word. In some cases, you may even represent the word divided into syllables so students can practice saying/reading the word. |
| 2. Associate the term with a picture, model, or diagram. | You can certainly provide any of these visual tools, but they are most meaningful and memorable when students draw the pictures or make their own connections. |

| Ways for Students to Process, Elaborate, and Practice Critical Content Vocabulary | Explanatory Notes for Teacher |
|---|---|
| 3. Write the meaning of the word in your own words. | Students will have multiple opportunities to review and revisit their original definitions and make corrections and additions. Attempt to guide students to an accurate definition, but do not dictate the definition to them. |
| 4. Act out the meaning of the word. | Not all terms can be represented by gestures, actions, or facial expressions, but when they can, this is a powerful way for students to acquire meanings. |
| 5. Write a sentence showing you know how to use the word correctly apart from its relationship to the content. | If students have difficulty writing sentences to show that they know the meaning, model the writing of "show you know" sentences. |
| 6. Discuss the word's meaning and relationship to content with a partner. | Whenever student pairs are sharing, be sure to monitor their discussions for accuracy and clarity. |
| 7. Hear the teacher use the word in the context of content input. | When you are presenting new content and you use the term, run your hand under a printed representation of the word. Anytime students can both hear the word spoken and see it in print, it is another opportunity to acquire an accurate meaning of the word. |
| 8. Read the word in internet articles. | Encourage students to look for the term online and make a note of where they encountered and read it. |
| 9. Read, spell, define, and write the word. | Using all of these processes enables students to acquire meanings more quickly. |
| 10. Complete a graphic organizer that shows various meanings of a word in other contexts. | If the term is a key concept of new content, construct a concept map on your classroom wall that explicitly shows the relationship between the key concept and all of its related terms. |
| 11. Write a question about the word's meaning. | Students may be able to write a simple definition in their own words but may have questions about the subtle nuances of a word. Encourage them to write their questions down in their vocabulary notebook. |
| 12. Use the word outside of class or document a sighting or hearing of the word on digital media. | There is a remarkable phenomenon that occurs when students are introduced to difficult words for the first time. They often become fascinated with a word and suddenly hear and see the word everywhere. When this happens, you will know that your students are becoming word conscious. |

Figure 3.2 displays six steps for introducing new content terms. Some of the content information found in this figure is described in more depth in the elementary classroom example found later in this technique.

**Figure 3.2: Six Steps for Introducing New Content Terms**

| Lesson Step | Example From Critical Content |
|---|---|
| 1. Give students a description, explanation, or example of the new terms. | Two terms used to describe the same set of acts passed by the British Parliament in 1774: the Intolerable Acts and the Coercive Acts. If something is intolerable, you cannot take it anymore. Who could not take it anymore? If something is coercive, you are trying to force someone to do something they do not want to do. Who was trying to force someone to do something? |
| 2. Ask students to restate the description, explanation, or example in their own words. | Describe which term applies to the acts from the British perspective and which term applies to the acts from the colonists' perspective. |
| 3. Ask students to draw a picture or create a graphic organizer to represent the term. | Student draws a picture of the colonists dumping over a million dollars (in today's economy) worth of tea into the Boston Harbor in protest. |
| 4. Have students periodically revise or add to the information in their vocabulary notebook. | After students have more content input and opportunities to discuss the word meanings, they revise their definitions to be more comprehensive. |
| 5. Periodically have students discuss the term with a partner. | What is the significance of these four acts the British parliament passed? Remind your partner about the meanings of the terms *intolerable* and *coercive*. |
| 6. Involve students in games or introduce a new graphic organizer to review and reinforce word meanings. | Construct word maps using the terms *intolerable* and *coercive*. Do a comparison activity with the two words. |

The six steps are adapted from Marzano & Pickering (2005). The examples are original to this guide.

# Revising Knowledge Using the Content Vocabulary Notebook

The pages of a content vocabulary notebook can be designed to suit your content and your students. Figure 3.3 displays a one-row sample of the notebook. There are four rows in the full-page version found in Resource: Descriptive Pattern. Each successive row provides evidence of a student's growing understanding of a key concept or term as recorded in her own words and as represented in a drawing or organizer the student has created or a photo or graphic retrieved from the internet.

**Figure 3.3: Sample of Content Vocabulary Revision Template**

| Meaning of the Term in My Own Words | My Visual Representation of the Term |
|---|---|
|  |  |

# Common Mistakes

Here are several of the common mistakes you can make when teaching your students how to revise knowledge using their content vocabulary notebooks:

- The teacher fails to plan for the revision of prior vocabulary learning at every stage of the learning process.

- The teacher fails to understand that neatness, accurate grammar usage, and accurate spelling are not essential for recording and representing knowledge. The goal of revising knowledge is for students to deepen their understanding of key critical content concepts through an ongoing revision process.

- The teacher fails to model strategies for revising prior learning about key content vocabulary.

- The teacher fails to take the time needed for multiple opportunities to review students' prior knowledge and revise or amend it.

- The teacher fails to create an environment in which revision is thought of as a powerful and important part of the learning process.

- The teacher fails to establish and then consistently implement procedures for managing content vocabulary notebooks to include allocated space for their storage and certain routines and allocated times for revising knowledge in the notebooks.

- The teacher fails to allow students the benefits of retention and deepening understandings of critical content by regulating and dictating to students what should or should not be included in their vocabulary notebook.

- The teacher fails to schedule opportunities for students to correct and amend knowledge in their notebooks in advance of summative assessments.

## Examples and Nonexamples of Revising Knowledge Using Content Vocabulary Notebooks or Templates

Following are two examples (one elementary and one secondary) and their corresponding nonexamples of revising prior learning using content vocabulary notebooks or templates. Recall Figure 1.7 from earlier in the guide that illustrates a possible learning sequence leading up to students revising their prior understanding of a concept.

### Elementary Example of Revising Knowledge

The learning target for this elementary example of revising knowledge using content vocabulary notebooks is *determine the meaning of general academic and domain-specific words or phrases in a text relevant to a grade 5 topic or subject area* (CCSS.ELA-Literacy.RI.4.4). The teacher introduces two new content terms to fifth-grade students who are studying events leading up to the writing of the Declaration of Independence: the *Coercive Acts* and the *Intolerable Acts*. In the organizer, the teacher has selected the terms *intolerable* and *coercive* to teach students about the events that followed the Boston Tea Party. The students are using full-page copies of the Content Vocabulary Revision Template displayed earlier in a shortened format in Figure 3.3.

Class, we've been studying a number of important events that happened in the Massachusetts Bay Colony leading up to the writing of the Declaration of Independence. Today we're going to focus on two terms that describe the same set of laws that the British Parliament passed in 1774. There were four different laws. The British called these laws the Coercive Acts, and the colonists called them the Intolerable Acts. An *act* is a law. If you understand the meanings of *intolerable* and *coercive*, you'll soon begin to figure out what led to the breakup between England and the colonies.

Don't take any notes right now. I want you to listen and focus on fixing the meanings of these two words in your minds: *coercive* and *intolerable*. If something is intolerable, you can't take it anymore. Who couldn't take what anymore? If something is coercive, it means that someone is trying to force you to do something you don't want to do. Now, think for a moment about something intolerable that you have experienced. The sound of all those wrong notes I'm hearing from my brother's trumpet while he's practicing is intolerable. I just can't stand it anymore. Or, think about something coercive that you have experienced—being forced to do something that you didn't want to do and maybe you felt you were being treated unfairly.

The British called the acts they passed coercive. They were trying to force the colonies into doing things they didn't want to do. The colonists called the acts intolerable. They were simply not going to stand for this kind of treatment. I want you to turn to your partner and talk about these two words. First talk about something that you find intolerable—something you just can't stand. Then talk with each other about how the word connects to England and the colonies. Who called the acts the Intolerable Acts, and who called the acts the Coercive Acts? Once you have finished sharing, read aloud with your partner the section in your textbook that describes exactly what the acts are and why they were passed. Once you finish your reading, tell your partner what you now know about these acts.

After students finish their reading, the teacher passes out a copy of the content vocabulary revision page to each student (Resource: Descriptive Pattern). He explains that the terms they are going to write about are *Coercive Acts* and *Intolerable Acts*. On the left side of the page, they are to write as much as they have learned about these acts. On the right side of the page, they are to draw a picture or graphic to represent something they want to remember about these acts. As the week progresses, the teacher adds additional content input, and students continue to process and elaborate. As they deepen their understanding of the terms, they acquire from the historical context a deeper understanding of the meanings of *intolerable* and *coercive*. Figures 3.4 and 3.5 are examples of first entries into a content vocabulary notebook.

### Elementary Nonexample

The learning target for this elementary nonexample of revising knowledge using content vocabulary notebooks is *determine the meaning of general academic and domain-specific words or phrases in a text relevant to a grade 5 topic or subject area* (CCSS.ELA-Literacy.RI.4.4). The nonexample teacher has high expectations that her students will begin to use their content vocabulary notebooks to revise their understandings of key concepts and terms. The students do a good job of making their first entries, but the teacher then loses track of time and is on to new content before students have a chance to revisit their entries. The goal of using content vocabulary notebooks is for students to acquire deeper meanings of difficult academic vocabulary. However, they need to make regular updates as they receive more input from the teacher.

**Figure 3.4: Sample First Entry into a Content Vocabulary Notebook**

| Meaning of the Term in My Own Words | My Visual Representation of the Term |
|---|---|
| If something is intolerable, it means that it's terrible and you can't stand it any longer.<br><br>If something is coercive, it means it's being forced on you. | <br><br>Coercive and intolerable |

**Figure 3.5: A Second Entry for a Content Vocabulary Notebook: Social Studies**

| Meaning of the Term in My Own Words | My Visual Representation of the Term |
|---|---|
| Intolerable describes something that is impossible to put up with. The acts the British Parliament passed went too far. They cannot be tolerated, the colonists said.<br><br>Coercive means using force or pressure of some kind to get people to do what you want them to do, usually against their will. The behavior of the colonists is out of control. We have to force them to do what we want and show them who is the boss here. | Boston Tea Party<br><br>British Parliament passes the Coercive Acts (called the Intolerable Acts by the colonists).<br><br>Other colonies rushed to help the colonists in Boston, and rather than the Coercive Acts working as they were intended, everybody got together to fight against the British. |

*Secondary Example of Revising Knowledge*
*Using Content Vocabulary Notebooks*

There are two learning targets for this secondary example of revising knowledge using content vocabulary notebooks. The first is *determine the meaning of symbols, key terms, and other domain-specific words and phrases as they are used in a specific scientific context relevant to grade 9–10 texts and topics* (CCSS.ELA-Literacy.RST.9-10.4). The second learning target is from science: *Use a model to illustrate how photosynthesis transforms light energy into stored chemical energy. Models could include diagrams, chemical equations, and conceptual models* (Next Generation Science Standards, HS-LSI-5).

The teacher has introduced the process of photosynthesis to his ninth-grade students over a several-day sequence of critical-content input and a variety of activities in which they have processed, elaborated, and recorded and represented their current understanding of photosynthesis on the first page of their content vocabulary revision notebook (Resource: Descriptive Pattern). They dated their first entries, and today the teacher asks them to revise their understanding of photosynthesis after reviewing their prior definition and prior visual representation.

Class, before you take your seats, please retrieve your content vocabulary notebooks. We are going to spend time revising the entries we made earlier in the week.

Look at the wall chart that lists the steps you should take in the process of revising your prior learning (see Figure 1.3 in Instructional Technique 1). Students have revised their prior learning about photosynthesis several times and today will make the final entry by summarizing their learning. Figure 3.6 is a sample of one student's Content Vocabulary Notebook page featuring photosynthesis.

**Figure 3.6: Sample Content Vocabulary Notebook: Photosynthesis**

| Meaning of the Term in My Own Words | My Visual Representation of the Term |
|---|---|
| Photosynthesis is something that happens in trees and plants. It involves water and air and sunshine. Chlorophyll in the leaves is also part of the process. The water gets to the trees and plants through their roots. | sun / light / carbon dioxide from the air / water |

| After Reviewing My Prior Definition | After Reviewing My Previous Visual |
|---|---|
| There are lots of chemical reactions going on during photosynthesis so I need to know more biology and chemistry to understand photosynthesis. | $6H_2O + 6CO_2 \xrightarrow{\text{Sunlight}} C_6H_{12}O_6 + 6O_2$  water + carbon dioxide $\xrightarrow{\text{Sunlight}}$ glucose + oxygen |

| After Reviewing My Prior Definition | After Reviewing My Previous Visual |
|---|---|
| Photosynthesis is how plants make their food. Photosynthesis is needed for life on earth. When we eat plants, we use the glucose. The oxygen that is released in the process goes into the air for us to breathe. | The reactants are water and carbon dioxide. The products are glucose and oxygen.  Reactants: water and carbon dioxide → glucose and oxygen : Products |

| My Final Definition of the Term | My Final Visual Representation |
|---|---|
| Photosynthesis is the process through which plants make their own food. It's important to use the word process to define photosynthesis. A process is a series of things that happen in nature. Photosynthesis happens in the chloroplast, an organelle. | Energy / chloroplast / CO₂ + water / sugar + oxygen |

Information about photosynthesis adapted from Photosynthesis Video. TV411 Tune in to Learning. Education Development Center, Inc.

*Secondary Nonexample of Revising Knowledge*
*Using a Content Vocabulary Notebook*

The content vocabulary notebooks of the nonexample teacher's students look quite different from those in the example classroom. The teacher has developed an impressive PowerPoint presentation filled with animated graphics and brand-new content information. From the teacher's perspective, there is so much material to cover and such a short time in which to bring students up to speed on this important content that he has allocated time for them to make only one entry in their notebooks. The teacher asks students to retrieve their notebooks and revise their prior learning. Students are confused both by the vast amount of information that has recently been presented and the knowledge revision process itself. They are unable to adequately revise their prior learning using the basics of knowledge revision.

## Determining If Students Can Revise Knowledge Using Content Vocabulary Notebooks

The following suggestions can help you determine if your students can revise their prior learning using content vocabulary notebooks:

- Students review previous vocabulary definitions and visual representations and then record and represent their revised knowledge. The teacher walks around and reads their entries to ensure students are recording correct information and also collects the notebooks to check that the entries are correct.

- Students work with partners to discuss how their understanding about key terms or concepts has changed since they made previous entries, while the teacher walks around and listens in on the conversations.

- After students revise knowledge in their content vocabulary notebooks, they close their notebooks and write one important piece of critical information on individual whiteboards and then hold them up. This activity requires students to retain the information in their short-term memories from their revisions long enough to affix it into their memories.

- Students complete an exit slip that answers a statement, such as "I used to think _____ about this topic, but now I understand _____."

Use the student proficiency scale for revising knowledge using content vocabulary notebooks shown in Table 3.1 to determine how your students are progressing in their ability to make additions and deletions to previous knowledge that deepen their understanding.

**Table 3.1: Student Proficiency Scale for Revising Knowledge Using Content Vocabulary Notebooks**

| Emerging | Fundamental | Desired Result |
|---|---|---|
| Students struggle with revising definitions and visual representation of key content vocabulary accurately in their notebooks.<br><br>Students may be unable to decide what information needs to be added or edited. | Students identify the parts of their definitions that were initially correct and/or incorrect.<br><br>Students review and add to their previous correct definitions of key content terms and correct misconceptions and mistakes from previous entries. | Students can successfully revise information in their content vocabulary notebooks, and using their notebooks, apply this knowledge to the overall unit of content learning. |

## Scaffold and Extend Instruction to Meet Students' Needs

Meeting the needs of your students may require designing lessons for both your struggling and higher-achieving students. In either case, your goal is to help students become more self-managed in your classroom as they revise knowledge using their content vocabulary notebooks. Below are some examples of each.

Scaffolding

- Determine if students need to receive more support during recording and representing of their learning following critical-input experiences.

- Meet with students to go over their content vocabulary notebooks and talk through the critical information to help students identify and correct misconceptions or add important information.

- Provide correct definitions specific to each entry that you want the students to review and revise.

- Provide peer support in the form of a helpful student who can assist the struggling students in recording and representing knowledge.

## Extending

- Ask students to create questions that will show they can make connections to other material or deeper learnings that will extend their knowledge.

- Ask students to reword their entries for a specific audience—for example, a much younger student, or a post on Facebook or Twitter.

- Ask students to develop a set of questions their classmates might use to help them more effectively review and revise their notebook entries.

## Instructional Technique 4

# REVISING KNOWLEDGE USING VISUAL TOOLS

Visual tools include a range of nonlinguistic representations: graphic organizers, graphs, charts, student drawings, digital depictions, PowerPoint presentations, and more. Consider the following ways that visual tools can help your students revise knowledge:

- Visual tools are adaptable to any discipline, content, or grade level.

- Visual tools are able to communicate complex concepts or summarize large chunks of text with fewer words, making them ideal for students who have strong visual and spatial skills but struggle with reading extensive texts.

- Visual tools can picture ideas graphically and spatially, making complex concepts and processes more understandable and memorable.

- Constructing a visual tool as one aspect of revising knowledge provides students with a structured framework into which they are able to organize or fit their knowledge. This experience often helps students identify gaps in their knowledge, which in turn leads them to make further revisions of knowledge, or even forces them to select a visual tool that is more compatible with the knowledge they are representing.

- Visual tools require that students separate key words and concepts before they begin filling in the circles and boxes.

- Visual tools require that students figure out the relationships between various concepts.

- Visual tools enable students to identify trivial or unimportant information more readily when they realize that what they thought was important does not flow into the organizer.

- Visual tools can be created with low-tech pen and paper or designed with computer software.

- Visual tools partner well with note-taking systems or academic notebooks, giving students ways to both represent and record knowledge.

- Visual tools can provide hands-on experiences with manipulatives and models that supplement teacher presentations and textbook readings.

## How to Effectively Implement Revising Knowledge Using Visual Tools

There are several guidelines to keep in mind as you plan for the effective implementation of revising knowledge using visual tools:

- Remember that the value of creating visual tools only accrues to the individuals who create them. You can use a lesson template to model how to construct a certain type of organizer, but do not think that the lessons *you* learned during the creation of that visual tool can automatically be conferred on your students through the reprographic ability of the office copier. The messiest drawing that represents new learning to a student is more powerful for that student than the flashiest PowerPoint his teacher creates. In using visual tools, the process is far more important than the product.

- Remember that you cannot possibly teach your students how to use all of the visual tools in the universe. Therefore, your first challenge is to examine a limited set of visual tools and then choose those that are likely to be most beneficial for your students and content. Develop simple one-page templates with clearly labeled frames for the set of visual tools you plan to use as staples in your classroom. Make them available to your students for revising prior learning.

- Remember that you cannot expect students to choose and complete graphic organizers from your classroom library of templates unless you have modeled the various tools for them using somewhat familiar critical content.

Table 4.1 shows a basic lesson for modeling how to use a visual tool to revise knowledge.

**Table 4.1: Lesson Plan for Teaching and Modeling a Visual Tool for Revising Knowledge**

| Lesson Step | Explanatory Notes |
|---|---|
| 1. Select a graphic organizer that will allow for representing current content. | Students are more likely to become familiar with organizers and how best to use them if you provide ample copies of various templates. |
| 2. Show students several models of the organizer (two well-constructed samples and two poorly done nonexamples). Explain the purpose of constructing this organizer and how it can be used to understand and remember critical content. | The power of excellent examples and nonexamples cannot be overstated. Students need to see what a good one looks like. The purpose of this process is not for them to acquire the information on the organizer that you or another student may have constructed, but inspect the types of words and phrases that comprise the contents of the organizer. |
| 3. Explain the various frames (labels) of the organizer, describing what kind of information needs to go into each specific section of the organizer. | In the beginning, students need clearly labeled frames to figure out what goes in the various boxes or circles. Always provide frames with organizers unless your students are prepared to create their own frames. |
| 4. Introduce a key word or concept from an upcoming unit of study and tell students you are going to model for them and think aloud about how you construct the organizer you have chosen. | For example, construct a concept map using key concepts from mathematics: fraction, division, reciprocal, divisor, dividend, and quotient, plus some properties from dividing fractions. |
| 5. Model for students how you test or try out possible words and ideas for the contents of the organizer. | Overcome any reluctance you may have to model and think aloud for your students. Be the cognitive master for your students. |
| 6. Post your completed organizer as a sample. Choose a different concept or topic, and ask a student volunteer to help you begin to construct it. Ask student partners to complete that organizer. | Post the students' organizers in the classroom. Debrief with students about conclusions regarding the organizers. |

# Common Mistakes

As with other techniques, there are some common mistakes you can make when directly teaching and modeling for your students the process of revising their knowledge using visual tools. Here are several ways this technique can go off course:

- The teacher fails to plan for revision of knowledge using visual tools in every stage of learning. This includes the need to check for correct understandings and make revisions during the progression of learning.

- The teacher fails to model revising strategies. Although students may be familiar with creating visuals or using graphic organizers, they may not be familiar with how to use those tools for revision. Teacher modeling or the provision of exemplars will help students have success with this process.

- The teacher fails to plan in advance regarding the availability and amount of manipulatives needed for the revision process.

- The teacher moves too quickly through the knowledge revision process. Students need adequate time to consider their misunderstandings and gaps and make those revisions.

- The teacher fails to provide opportunities to deepen or practice knowledge before having students move to the revision process. Students cannot revise knowledge they do not have. Knowledge revision is impossible to implement effectively unless students engage in sufficient deepening activities, such as multiple exposures to process declarative knowledge and multiple opportunities to practice procedural knowledge.

- The teacher fails to monitor students for deepening understandings of concepts throughout the revision process to make sure the revised information is accurate.

## Examples and Nonexamples of Revising
## Knowledge Using Visual Tools

Following are two examples (one elementary and one secondary) and their corresponding nonexamples for revising knowledge using visual tools. As you read, think about experiences you have had in your classroom or observed in colleagues' classrooms. Consider the common mistakes and note how the example teachers cleverly avoid them and the nonexample teachers miss the mark with their lack of understanding of how to use this technique. Also, think about how a teacher might monitor for the desired result of revising knowledge.

### *Elementary Example of Revising Knowledge Using Visual Tools*

This elementary example illustrates how to revise knowledge using visual tools. The learning target is *fluently multiply and divide within 100, using strategies such as the relationship between multiplication and division (e.g., knowing that 8 × 5 = 40, one knows 40 ÷ 5 = 8) or properties of operations* (CCSS-Mathematics.3.OA.7).

The teacher begins her lesson.

> Students, I am so proud of all your hard work. We have been working with multiplying one-digit numbers that end in multiples of 10. We have used 10 through 90, and all of those multiples end in 0. Yesterday we did a quick check for accuracy, and today we are going to revise our mistakes. You all know that is the way we do things in our classroom. I am handing back the corrected assessment so that you can see your mistakes.

She previously introduced the standards-based learning goal and scale to the students, using instructional strategies to plan lessons and scaffold and teach the learning goal. As students began to practice and deepen knowledge, she had them self-select some of the problems in the book, work on problems in pairs, and model some problems using manipulatives in front of the class. She called about five students up to use the manipulatives to demonstrate the self-selected problems. She also assigned homework, revised homework mistakes with the students, and then gave the ten-item assessment.

She found that the majority of her students were able to correctly execute eight problems out of ten. However, she noticed after analyzing the assessment that most of the mistakes students made involved the 70s, 80s, and 90s. She also knew from past math work that the single-digit numbers of 7, 8, and 9 were the most challenging for students to multiply. It was not that they did not know how to multiply using numbers with a zero at the end; it was that some students were still struggling with multiplying 7s, 8s, and 9s. Instead of asking students to redo the problems they missed, she paired students and gave each pair a bag of hard black beans. She asked them to look at the problems that they missed and together demonstrate the problem visually with the beans. In other words, if they missed 7 × 6, they would put seven beans down six times in rows under the first row. If they had to manually count the beans, they could. After they saw the product, they were asked to go back and revise their work, explaining how the beans helped them solve the problem. For students who earned 100% on the formative assessment, she asked them to demonstrate a different way to solve the problem.

### Elementary Nonexample of Revising Using Visual Tools

The following elementary nonexample is based on the same grade level and standards-based learning goal as the previous example.

> I am handing back your assessment from yesterday. Your score is at the top. We need more work on multiplying one-digit numbers by multiples of 10. I do not know why you seemed to be able to get some of these problems correct and then still missed a few. I am handing out ten more problems like the ones you did on the assessment. Work alone and do these ten problems.

Our nonexample teacher corrected the assessment but failed to identify patterns or analyze her students' mistakes. She did not expect students to determine why they made the mistakes they did or have a plan for how to guide them to revising their understanding of the process of multiplication.

She believes more practice will help them learn how to do the problems. The teacher does not use visual tools to help her students revise or enhance their prior learning.

*Secondary Example of Revising Knowledge Using Visual Tools*

The learning target for this example is *interpret and compute quotients of fractions, and solve word problems involving division of fractions by fractions* (CCSS-Math.Content.6.NSA.1). The sixth-grade teacher is introducing the division of fractions by fractions. The content example is adapted from Montis & Pell (2010). The teacher introduces his lesson this way:

> Class, today we are going to begin working on the division of fractions. Now, if you have parents who work with math on a daily basis, and you ask them what the rule for dividing fractions is—that is, the standard algorithm for dividing fractions—they would quickly tell you "invert the divisor and multiply by the reciprocal, or change to divide and multiply by the reciprocal." For those who don't speak "math," it sounds almost like a foreign language. But, when you know the definition of division, properties of multiplication, and properties of equality, you will not only be able to speak "math," but you will be able to understand the math.

The teacher then works out two word problems on the board:

1. Your mother told you to get five dollars in quarters. How many quarters should you bring back?

2. Dad told you to give the chickens four pails of feed. You are strong enough to carry only half a pail at a time. How many trips do you need to make?

> You would probably solve the first problem by considering that there are four quarters in a dollar. And then since you have $5 and 5 × 4 = 20, we would have twenty quarters. For the second problem, you would consider that there are two halves in each pail so that two trips are needed for one pail. And then since four pails of feed are needed and 4 × 2 = 8, you would need to make eight trips. But, I want you to use the fraction strips to help you visualize this process.

The teacher gives each group of four students some fraction strips and asks them to cut the strips into appropriate sections to illustrate how to solve the two problems. The students readily understand that one fraction strip containing four sections represents $1 and five strips represents $20. Likewise, in the second problem, a fraction slip with two sections represents one pail, and eight trips would be needed to carry all of the chicken feed. During the last step of the lesson, the teacher represents the two problems another way to show that the solution suggested by the visual tools can demonstrate the common rule for the division of fractions:

$$1)\ 5 \div \tfrac{1}{4} = 5 \times 4 = 20$$

and

$$2)\ 4 \div \tfrac{1}{2} = 4 \times 2 = 8.$$

These problems demonstrate the common rule: invert the divisor and multiply by the reciprocal. During upcoming lessons, the teacher plans to use these same problems to demonstrate the reasoning behind the common rule. To conclude the lesson, the teacher asks students to complete a knowledge revision template shown in Figure 4.1 about how the lesson has made them revise their prior understanding of dividing a fraction by another fraction.

**Figure 4.1: Revision Template for Dividing Fractions**

| Used to Think | Now I Know | What I Still Do Not Know |
|---|---|---|
| List of some initial understandings.<br><br>· *I didn't think you could divide one fraction by another. I thought you could just divide a whole number by a fraction.*<br><br>· *Before using the fraction strips, I had no idea at all how to divide a fraction by a fraction.* | How those understandings in the left-hand column changed—additional knowledge or a misunderstanding that was corrected.<br><br>· *Now I can visualize how the process takes place, and that makes it much less confusing to me.*<br><br>· *I still have questions about how the whole process of inverting the divisor and multiplying by the reciprocal works.* | Things I need more information about:<br><br>· *I'm still uncertain about what the terms divisor and reciprocal actually mean.*<br><br>· *Will I have to use fraction strips to do all of my problems?* |

*Secondary Nonexample of Revising Knowledge Using Visual Tools*

The secondary nonexample teacher is focused on the same learning target and selects the same problem set, demonstrating the solution of both problems with fraction strips on the overhead projector. Students seem to readily understand the solutions and have no questions, so he decides to move forward without giving students the opportunity to manipulate the fraction strips. When he reads through the revision templates his students completed, he finds that they are more confused and frustrated about fraction division after his lesson than they were before. He goes back to his desk to begin planning a new lesson, one that actually gives his students opportunities to manipulate visual tools.

## Determining If Students Can Revise Knowledge Using Visual Tools

As the majority of your students become more skilled at revising prior knowledge using visual tools, you will have increased opportunities to identify the information, concepts, and procedures they did not understand the first time they were introduced. To find out how well students revise misinformation, fill in gaps, and make corrections, assemble a tool kit of monitoring tasks designed to fit your grade and/or content area. Here are some ways that effective teachers monitor their students' progress:

- As students work with their visual tools independently or in groups, the teacher walks around and checks on their new understanding.

- While students are working on revising their prior learning, the teacher asks questions of students to determine the reasoning behind their revisions.

- Students display their visual tools by arranging them on their desks or holding up a whiteboard or response card for the teacher to see.

- Students are paired to either share their new understandings or explain why they made a certain mistake. The teacher circulates and listens to the discussions taking place.

- Students place a star or happy face in a bright color near a newly corrected revision. The teacher can quickly spot or scan the corrections.

- Students write their new understandings or do one of the corrected problems on a classroom visual enabling the teacher to quickly ascertain their understanding.

Table 4.2 contains a student proficiency scale for revising knowledge using visual tools. Use and adapt as needed to determine how your students are progressing on the scale. Think of additional ways you can monitor students for the achievement of proficiency levels on this scale.

**Table 4.2: Student Proficiency Scale for Revising Knowledge Using Visual Tools**

| Emerging | Fundamental | Desired Result |
|---|---|---|
| Students revise mistakes inaccurately using the visual tool.<br><br>Students may still be unable to decide what information is needed to correct misunderstandings. | Students identify understandings that were initially correct and/or incorrect.<br><br>Students can use the visual tool accurately to revise basic misunderstandings and deepen understanding. | Students can successfully use a visual tool to revise information in the lesson and deepen understanding, and can make extensions and applications to the learning. They are able to depict or visually represent their new learning. |

# Scaffold and Extend Instruction to Meet Students' Needs

For some students, connecting visual tools to revising knowledge will be a challenge, and for others, an extension activity will be needed. You will identify those students as you monitor your class for the desired result of this strategy.

## Scaffolding

- Develop a bulletin board showing visual tools and revisions that other students made.

- Develop picture keys for showing steps to use in a revision such as found in Figure 1.3 earlier in this guide.

- Post a selection of visual tools that students can choose from when they need to revise prior learning.

## Extending

When your students have readily mastered the use of a wide range of visual tools, they are ready for a challenge. Following are some ways to extend their understandings:

- Prioritize or categorize the new learning in list form.

- Create an original visual tool to represent learning in a different way.

- Help a partner identify mistakes and give him suggestions for understanding the material.

## Instructional Technique 5

# REVISING KNOWLEDGE USING WRITING TOOLS

Revising knowledge using various writing tools should not be confused with the process of revising written work in English language arts (ELA) classrooms. The writing tools to be used for revising knowledge are the means to a much different end than the revision process in ELA. The purpose of revision in ELA is to improve and polish a specific product, acquiring procedures to write to various prompts and revise to perfection.

The purpose of writing in the context of revising knowledge is not for students to produce polished essays, but wrestle with words and ideas to figure out what they know and do not know, and then seek out additional knowledge. This is not to say that increased opportunities to revise knowledge through the process of writing will not gradually improve the writing skills and fluency of even the most reluctant writers. In fact, the students most likely to benefit from this technique are those who have a great deal to write about, but need some tools to guide them as well as permission to focus more on the revision of knowledge and less on grammar, spelling, and writing techniques. A phrase that is sometimes used in discussions about the reading/writing connection is *"writing in the service of reading comprehension."* That phrase describes what happens when students write about something they have read: their understanding or reading comprehension improves, sometimes dramatically. However, in the context of revising prior learning, you will teach and model for students the use of *"writing in the service of deepening their content learning."*

# How to Effectively Implement Revising Knowledge Using Writing

There are three sets of writing tools to assist you and your students in the effective implementation of revising knowledge: 1) a set of cognitive processing tools that emphasize writing in the service of content learning: summarizing and concluding; 2) a set of streamlined tools that provide scaffolds for students who struggle with writing such as quick-writes, sentence stems, exit tickets, and interactive notebooks; and 3) a set of student-driven writing projects that showcase students' more mature abilities to revise knowledge: a) student-generated assessments and b) self-selected writing for revision.

# Revising Knowledge Using Summarizing and Concluding

Summarizing and concluding are cognitive processes that, when focused on a specific aspect of knowledge revision, serve to deepen students' understanding of critical content. Figure 5.1 defines these two processes to clearly differentiate them. These processes are essential to reading, thinking, and writing, but the emphasis in this technique is on the thinking/writing process.

**Figure 5.1: Definitions of Summarizing and Concluding in the Context of Revising Knowledge**

| Thinking/Writing Process | Working Definition |
|---|---|
| Summarizing | Identifying the most important information (central ideas and key supporting details) and writing about them in your own words. |
| Concluding | Making a decision about information you have seen, heard, and read during various parts of the content-input process. Concluding during the revising knowledge process must be based on substantial evidence that is seen, heard, or read during that process. |

Definitions adapted from McEwan (2004, 2007) and McEwan-Adkins & Burnett (2012).

## Summarizing

Summarizing is a cognitive process that is essential to learning. In the context of revising knowledge, summarizing is a very powerful tool. A more elaborate definition of summarizing in the context of revising prior learning is *writing a sentence or two at a certain point in the learning process that tells what is most important about that newly acquired knowledge.* Brown and Day (1983) define summarizing as "the ability to recursively work on information to render it as succinctly as possible" (p. 1). Summarizing in the service of revising prior learning demands recursive work in which students keep coming back as many times as needed to rewrite and rework what they first wrote about some aspect of critical content. This will allow them to create a more accurate and comprehensive version of their learning. Therefore, summarizing in the service of revising prior learning is not the preparation of a final summative product, but rather a collection of short summary statements students make about what they know so far. There will be no grade for the writing product, per se. The grade, if any, will be reflected in the deeper understanding that students acquire.

Figure 5.2 illustrates how you can teach and model for students how to use summarizing in the service of knowledge revision. If you have not previously taught and modeled for your students how to write a summary, teach that process in a stand-alone lesson.

**Figure 5.2: Teaching and Modeling Summarizing in the Service of Knowledge Revision**

| Step in the Knowledge Revision Process Using Summarizing | Explanatory Information for the Teacher |
|---|---|
| 1. Acquire some knowledge to revise. | Many different classroom activities can masquerade as knowledge revision. You and your students can think you are revising knowledge well in advance of knowing enough about the content to even revise it. Recall Figure 1.7 in Instructional Technique 1 that enumerated the various parts of the learning process that must take place before students will be ready to revise knowledge. |
| 2. Prepare a template on which students will summarize their current understanding of content learning. | Your students can use academic notebooks, interactive notebooks, a revision template, or any other type of form you devise. However, the form shown in Figure 5.3 specifically focuses on summarizing in the ongoing revision of knowledge. |
| 3. Explain and model the three steps of summarizing what they know so far:<br><br>• Think about the first chunk of new learning that you acquired from a combination of a) listening to the teacher's presentation, b) reading your textbook, c) talking with your partner about the new learning, or d) making a drawing or diagram.<br><br>• Write down the main idea of the first chunk of learning and one or two supporting details.<br><br>• Succinctly combine or blend the most important information in your own words. | Explain to students that the summaries they will write will be like a snapshot of what they know so far.<br><br>Talk about how parents sometimes take pictures of their children on the first day of every school year: Why do you think they do that? To see how their children have grown and changed from one year to the next. The same thing is true of your understanding of a subject. The first time you learn about something, you may know just a little bit. But as you read in your textbook, hear the teacher explain more, and think about the subject more, you learn more. |

| Step in the Knowledge Revision Process Using Summarizing | Explanatory Information for the Teacher |
|---|---|
| 4. Ask students to take mental snapshots about how much they know about the content on any given day. | Display a blank copy of the snapshot summary template shown in Figure 5.3. Explain that each time students are ready to revise knowledge, they will follow the steps taught in Instructional Technique 1 to review their prior understanding, identify and correct any mistakes, identify gaps in knowledge and fill in the gaps, decide on any new information to include, and as needed explain the reasons for their changes. You may want to postpone this final step until the very end of the unit when students will summarize what they believed about a key concept or term at the beginning of instruction and what they now know to be true. |
| 5. Select a content topic with which students are familiar to model writing two or three summary statements. | Endeavor to show a progression and deepening of your understanding as you write your statements in each succeeding box, and stop between each statement to think aloud about what new learning you acquired that enabled you to write a more complete snapshot summary. |
| 6. Give each student a blank copy of the snapshot summary template. Direct them to write their first snapshot summary in the upper left-hand box of the template and write the date you have in your model. | A blank copy of the snapshot summary template for use in your classroom can be found in Resource: Snapshot Summary Template. |
| 7. Tell students to write just one sentence that contains something important they have learned about the key concept this far. | Explain to students that you are going to collect this first page in their snapshot album. Tell them that if they think about what they wrote and want to add some new information later, they should write it down in their notebook, and tomorrow they will have a chance to revise their summary. |
| 8. Have students work with their assigned partners to read what they have written. | |

**Figure 5.3: Snapshot Summary Form**

| Snapshot Summary 1<br>Date _____ | Snapshot Summary 2<br>Date _____ |
| --- | --- |
| | |

The power of the summary statements your students will write is derived from the fact that they represent a running record or cumulative historical statement of their acquisition of content knowledge. If their summary statements are not increasingly more accurate, complete, and meaningful, either the students are not learning, or they are not taking the knowledge revision process seriously. Following are some evaluation questions you might ask your students as you conference over the notebooks:

- Does your snapshot summary tell what's most important about the content you've learned so far?

- Does your snapshot summary have the most important words about the content you've learned so far?

- Is your snapshot summary in your own words?

- Is your snapshot summary short?

## Concluding

Concluding is the second thinking/writing process that can be used by your students to revise prior learning. *Generalizing* is a related word that is sometimes used as a synonym for *concluding*. However, the dictionary definition of *generalizing* is more encompassing in that to make a generalization, you must engage in some inferential thinking. In the process of revising knowledge, you want students to stick to the facts as they draw their conclusions. Concluding requires a different level of thinking and may be one of the ways you can extend writing in the service of knowledge revision to more advanced students. Figure 5.4 is a template for students to record their snapshot conclusions and evidence. Figure 5.5 contains a set of steps for teaching and modeling concluding to your students.

**Figure 5.4: Snapshot Conclusion Template**

| Snapshot Conclusion 1 Date _____ | Evidence for Snapshot Conclusion 1 |
|---|---|
| | |

**Figure 5.5: Teaching and Modeling Concluding in the Service of Knowledge Revision**

| Step in the Knowledge Revision Process Using Concluding | Explanatory Information |
|---|---|
| 1. Acquire some knowledge to revise. | Take care to identify in your own mind as well as in the minds of your students the difference between the activities that take place during the acquisition of knowledge as enumerated in Figure 1.7 found in Instructional Technique 1. If you have not taught a chunk of critical content and your students have not had opportunities to process, elaborate, or practice, they will be unable to step back from that process and make an initial entry that draws some conclusion about their learning to that point. |
| 2. Prepare a template on which students will draw a conclusion about their current understanding of content learning. | Your students can use academic notebooks, interactive notebooks, a revision template, or any other type of form you devise. However, the form shown in Figure 5.4 specifically focuses on drawing a conclusion in the ongoing revision of knowledge. |

*(Continued on next page)*

**(Figure 5.5, continued)**

| Step in the Knowledge Revision Process Using Concluding | Explanatory Information |
|---|---|
| 3. Explain and model the three steps of drawing a conclusion about what students know so far:<br><br>• Think about the first chunk of new learning that you acquired from a) listening to the teacher's presentation, b) reading your textbook, c) talking with your partner about the new learning, or d) making a drawing or diagram.<br><br>• Write down the most important evidence that you read or heard.<br><br>• Decide what this evidence means about the topic, and write your conclusion on the template. | Explain to students that the conclusions they will write will be like a snapshot of what they have concluded so far. As they learn more facts and have more evidence, their conclusions might need to be revised.<br><br>Talk about how parents sometimes take pictures of their children on the first day of every school year: Why do you think they do that? To see how their children have grown and changed from one year to the next. The same thing is true of your understanding of a subject. The first time you learn about something, you may know just a little bit. But as you read in your textbook, hear the teacher explain more, and think about the subject more, you learn more. |
| 4. Select a content topic with which students are familiar to model writing a conclusion about critical content. | Display a blank copy of the snapshot conclusion template shown in Figure 5.4, and write your conclusion. Explain that each time students are ready to revise knowledge, they will follow the steps they learned in Instructional Technique 1. |
| 5. Model thinking about your conclusion as you contemplate writing a second conclusion. | Endeavor to show a progression and deepening of your understanding as you write your statements in each succeeding box and stop between each statement to think aloud about what new learning you acquired that enabled you to write a new conclusion. |
| 6. Give each student a blank copy of the snapshot conclusion template. Direct the students to write their first snapshot conclusion in the upper left-hand box of the template and write the date as you have in your model. | Tell students to draw a conclusion based on the facts you have presented to them this far. The conclusion has to contain something important that they have learned about the specific content they are studying. |
| 7. Have students work with their assigned partners to read what they have written. | Explain to students that you are going to collect this first page in their snapshot album. Tell them that if they think about what they wrote and want to add some new information later, they should write it down in their notebook, and tomorrow they will have a chance to revise their summary. |

# Revising Knowledge Using Streamlined Writing Tools

Streamlined writing tools provide scaffolds to students who struggle with writing. This set of tools is also helpful for a quick formative assessment of whether certain groups of students are confused and how you might adjust your lesson plan to clarify confusion. However, the overriding purpose of using these processes is for students to record their thinking about critical content at a specific point in time; they will have an opportunity to revise it once they have acquired additional facts or information. The knowledge has to be written and revised by students, and for that to happen, there must be a place where you or students keep track of this information.

## Sentence Stems

Sentence stems, sometimes called sentence starters, are helpful for students who are stuck about what to write in their notebooks and templates. Give struggling students a copy of Figure 5.6 to keep in their notebooks. When you ask students to take out their notebooks to do some knowledge revision, their chart will be handy. Create a chart for your classroom using these stems and/ or others you have collected.

**Figure 5.6: Sentence Stems for Revision**

| Sentence Stem for Revision | Student's Response |
| --- | --- |
| I learned that . . . | |
| Something I have learned is . . . | |
| I noticed that . . . | |
| I changed my thinking about this concept when . . . | |
| I still don't understand . . . | |
| I used to think . . . but now I think . . . | |

## Quick-Writes and Quick-Draws

Quick-writes and quick-draws are an excellent tool for revising knowledge in the primary grades, where they can be used in any content area to develop writing fluency, build the habit of reflection, and assess student thinking. In a quick-write, students respond in a specified amount of time to an open-ended question or prompt the teacher provided. If you use academic or interactive notebooks, ask students to do a quick-write to record their knowledge or a quick-draw to represent their knowledge. Quick-draws are an excellent tool for revising knowledge in primary classrooms.

# Revising Knowledge Using Student-Driven Writing

## Student-Generated Questions

One way for students to revise their knowledge is by generating possible test questions related to critical content. For example, writing multiple-choice questions can be a challenging way to revise their prior learning and build confidence about the concepts for which they have written questions. Student-generated questions can be recorded in students' vocabulary or academic notebooks, or you can prepare a template for students to use that could be used in a small group discussion.

The question/answer quadrant in Figure 5.7 describes four types of questions students can record in their notebooks.

**Figure 5.7: Question/Answer Quadrant**

| Quadrant 1 | Quadrant 2 |
|---|---|
| In the upper left-hand quadrant, have students write a factual question for which the answer can usually be found very quickly in a specific part of the text, in the glossary of the textbook, or online via a digital device.<br><br>What is the first step in passing a bill? | This second type of question found in the upper right-hand quadrant is one for which students need to look in several different places in their textbook as well as other printed and digital resources. There is no one place in which the entire answer can be found. Students will need to synthesize and summarize their findings to answer the question.<br><br>How many and which committees in the House of Representatives and Senate held hearings on various versions of the Patient Protection and Affordable Care Act? |
| **Quadrant 3** | **Quadrant 4** |
| This question is inferential in nature, and the students who are asking and answering this type of question will need to exercise higher-level thinking skills.<br><br>Why was it so difficult for the Patient Protection and Affordable Care Act to be passed? | This question requires students to bring more of their personal experiences and feelings to answering the question.<br><br>What do you think should happen in Washington to speed up the process of passing bills into laws? |

Adapted from McEwan (2004).

Periodically, students can quiz each other using the questions they have written. For students who need support in asking questions as part of revising their prior learning, see the various sets of prompts in Figure 5.8.

**Figure 5.8: Questioning Prompts to Use in Revising Knowledge**

| Cause/Effect Question Prompts |
|---|
| What caused _____ to happen? |
| What are the consequences of _____? |
| What is the effect of _____? |
| How does _____ affect _____? |
| What do you hypothesize will be the outcome of _____? |

| Compare/Contrast Prompts |
|---|
| How are _____ and _____ alike? |
| Compare _____ and _____ with regard to _____. |
| What are the similarities between _____ and _____? |
| How would you contrast _____ and _____? |
| How are _____ and _____ different? |

| Evaluation Prompts |
|---|
| Which is best: _____ or _____? Why? |
| What is your opinion of _____? |
| What are the strengths and weaknesses of _____? |
| State if you agree or disagree with this statement: _____. Support your answer. |

| Recall Prompts |
|---|
| What are the different kinds of _____ described in this article? |
| What are the important _____ of _____? |
| What happened first in the story? |
| What are some characteristics of _____? |
| Tell about the sequence of events in this historical event. |
| How does the story end? |

Adapted from McEwan (2004).

## Student-Generated Assessments

"Perhaps the most powerful and underutilized type of assessment is student-generated assessment. As the name indicates, with this type of assessment, students propose tasks that will demonstrate their knowledge of a specific topic" (Marzano, 2010, p. 75). Students can use this type of assessment to demonstrate how they have revised their knowledge in substantial and more dramatic ways to give evidence to move from one level of proficiency to the next. If they understand the critical content and revise their knowledge, they will write or create assessments that will demonstrate that deeper understanding. Writing an assessment as a culmination of revising knowledge also gives students a sense of pride and accomplishment in their own learning. Students can "prove" that they have cleared up any misconceptions and revised their own knowledge when they write or create their own assessments. Student-generated assessments could include 1) writing a book review of a content-specific book demonstrating writing proficiency as well as the content knowledge needed to understand and critique the book, 2) building a model or constructing a complex concept map to demonstrate a deeper understanding of the content, or 3) selecting a historical topic and writing to advance some specific claims supported by evidence from historical research.

## Self-Selected Writing for Revision

With this method, students choose to write about a topic or answer a question about the topic to show they have deepened their understanding about the topic. An example of this is as follows: A student decides to take what she learned about the steps in solving an equation and write an expository piece describing these steps. If indeed the student accomplishes this self-selected writing, she will have demonstrated deepened understanding.

# Common Mistakes

Following are some common mistakes to avoid when implementing knowledge revision using writing tools:

- The teacher fails to model the writing strategies for knowledge revision. Students do not intuitively know how to revise for real learning using writing.

- The teacher insists that the writing be grammatically correct.

- The teacher fails to give students time to think when using more extensive and challenging activities.

- The teacher fails to establish a way of tracking students' knowledge acquisition in a meaningful way so as to judge if the technique is achieving its desired result.

- The teacher fails to monitor students to check on whether the knowledge revision using various writing tools is actually deepening students' understanding of critical content.

## Examples and Nonexamples of Revising Knowledge Using Writing

The following are examples and nonexamples of how the technique of revising knowledge through writing might be used in elementary and secondary classrooms. Consider several ways you might monitor for the desired effect in these examples.

### Elementary Example of Revising Knowledge Using Writing

The learning target for this example is based on two standards: *explain events, procedures, ideas, or concepts in a historical, scientific, or technical text, including what happened and why, based on specific information in the text* (CCSS-Literacy.RI.4.3) and *identify the major components of the digestive system and summarize the digestion process* (Objective 4.01, North Carolina Essential Standards). A fourth-grade class is studying digestion, and the teacher plans to use a writing tool to help her students pay more attention to their learning as they revise their prior learning. She has previously provided several content-input segments, and students have had multiple opportunities to process with their classmates and to record and represent their understanding in a variety of ways. Earlier the teacher modeled for them how to write snapshot summaries, and they wrote their first ones on their own snapshot summary page. Today, they are going to review what they wrote and "take" another snapshot summary showing how their learning is progressing. Throughout the week, the teacher is delighted by the progress her students are making. Figure 5.9 is a sample of one of her students' snapshot summary albums. She wants them to review all of the summaries they have written and evaluate them using these questions:

- Does your snapshot summary tell what's most important about the content you've learned so far?

- Does your snapshot summary have the most important words about the content you've learned so far?

- Is your snapshot summary written in your own words?

- Is your snapshot summary short?

**Figure 5.9: Snapshot Summary Album of the Digestive Process**

| Snapshot Summary 1 <br>Date Mon., 10-27<br><br>Digestion is a process that actually starts in the mouth when the teeth chew up food, and saliva starts to break down starches in food into sugars. | Snapshot Summary 2 <br>Date Wed., 10-29<br><br>If we don't chew our food properly, it will interfere with the process of digestion. It takes seven seconds for food in the mouth to go down a tube called the esophagus. |
|---|---|
| Snapshot Summary 3 <br>Date Fri., 10-31<br><br>There are muscles in the esophagus, and they squeeze the chewed-up food through to the stomach. This part of digestion is called peristalsis. | Snapshot Summary 4 <br>Date Tues., 11-4<br><br>There are a bunch of different things that happen in the stomach, almost too many to write about here. There are many different parts of the body helping to digest the food. |
| Snapshot Summary 5 <br>Date Wed., 11-5<br><br>Digestion is a very complicated process, and it's important to eat healthy food so that all the parts can work together to build new cells, repair what's wrong with us, and get nutrients into our blood. | Snapshot Summary 6 <br>Date Fri., 11-7<br><br>The human body is amazing because it takes the food I eat and turns it into the nutrients I need. If I don't watch what I eat and pay attention to my digestion, I could get indigestion like my grandma. Her digestive system no longer works very well. |

*Elementary Nonexample*

The teacher in the elementary nonexample is aiming at the same learning target and focuses on the digestive process. She decides that modeling the snapshot summary process would not be a good use of instructional time, believing that most of her students will be able to write the summary with only a brief explanation. She also does not consistently have students write in their "summary album." She has read some of the summaries, and they have not been that good. The lack of appropriate modeling and opportunities for guided practice for the students in using the technique has undermined a potentially effective lesson.

## Secondary Example of Revising Knowledge Through Writing

The learning target of this secondary example is to *identify key steps in a text's description of a process related to history/social studies, e.g., how a bill becomes law* (CCSS.ELA-Literacy.RH.6.83). A sixth-grade social studies teacher is teaching his students the process for how a bill becomes a law. The social studies text presents a very straightforward list of the steps, but the teacher wants his students to deepen their understanding of the process. To illustrate the process, he selects a law that has already passed Congress: a law dealing with health care. He has students do research on the internet to find out precise dates, individuals, and issues surrounding the law. He wants students to answer the questions raised by the various steps of the process. The teacher allocates about twenty minutes a day for students to work on internet searches to find materials about the health care bill. Students discover that the bill passed on January 5, 2010, and the president signed it into law on March 23, 2010. It was numbered H.R. 3590, and the official name is the Patient Protection and Affordable Care Act. There were seven different versions of the bill, and several committees from both the House of Representatives and the Senate worked on trying to get agreement between both houses of Congress. Each day after their research period, students make an entry in their snapshot conclusion page of their interactive notebook. They record the date in the box on the left, in which they are writing their conclusion, and in the box on the right, they write the evidence they found in their search that supports their conclusion. Figure 5.10 is an example of one student's snapshot conclusions regarding how a bill becomes a law.

**Figure 5.10: Sample Snapshot Conclusions: How a Bill Becomes a Law**

| Snapshot Conclusion 1 Date *11-5-14*  | Evidence for Snapshot Conclusion 1  |
|---|---|
| *After reading in the textbook about how a bill becomes a law, it sounded like a pretty straightforward and simple process. I've concluded that this was a very argumentative process, and the bill ended up being nothing like what it was originally intended to be.* | *Seven different versions of the bill were written.*<br><br>*Multiple committees of senators and representatives tried to work out something that everybody could agree to.*<br><br>*The bill has many amendments that seem to have nothing to do with actual patient protection and health care.* |
| Snapshot Conclusion 2 Date *11-6-14*  | Evidence for Snapshot Conclusion 2  |
| *After more reading about the passage of the Affordable Care Act, I've concluded that the representatives and senators don't often really represent their constituents.* | *Hundreds of thousands of dollars from various lobbyists and companies were spent to convince senators and representatives to vote for the version of the bill and amendments that would be most favorable to the lobbyists and companies.* |

### *Secondary Nonexample of Revising Knowledge Through Writing*

This secondary nonexample is based on the same learning target. The teacher did not feel that she could give her students the time to look for information about a specific bill on the internet and decided to summarize the information herself and present it during a twenty-minute content-input segment. She inadvertently communicated her own conclusions to students, depriving them of the opportunities to wrestle with the content and write their own snapshot conclusions.

# Determining If Students Can Revise Knowledge Through Writing

You will only know that revising knowledge through writing is having the desired effect if you intentionally monitor students' knowledge revision using writing. Here are some ways to keep track of your students' progress:

- Walk around reading written revisions and touching base with as many individuals, pairs, or groups as possible.

- Collect students' snapshot summaries and conclusions to determine their depth of understanding.

- Ask students to read their revisions to their partners or in groups, and listen and interject as you walk around the classroom.

- Use any form of technology or software that will help you quickly and easily see revisions students are making using writing. Post a revision question on their computers via the classroom website, and expect students to respond electronically.

Table 5.1 contains a student proficiency scale for revising knowledge through writing. Use this to help you monitor the level of success each student is having with this technique. That level of success is the desired result of this strategy.

**Table 5.1: Student Proficiency Scale for Revising Knowledge Through Writing**

| Emerging | Fundamental | Desired Result |
|---|---|---|
| Students struggle with writing a snapshot summary, quick-write, note, or exit ticket that describes or explains the revised skill or knowledge.<br><br>Students may still be unable to decide what information is needed to correct misunderstandings. | Students identify understandings that were initially correct and/or incorrect.<br><br>Students can write about and clarify their misunderstandings using the writing tool the teacher chooses that is appropriate for the content. | Using the writing tool the teacher chooses or a writing tool of the students' own choosing, students can apply the knowledge using concepts or make other links by extending and connect information to real-world settings. |

# Scaffolding and Extending

Meeting the needs of the diverse students in your classroom requires that you adapt your instruction. Here are some ideas for scaffolding and extending your instruction.

## Scaffolding

When you are having difficulty with one or a small group of students who do not seem be able to revise their understanding through writing, it may help to do the following:

- Model the processes of summarizing and concluding using easier content.

- Make sure you have identified the "must haves" that need revision. The must haves can be defined as the absolutely nonnegotiable parts of the standard being taught.

- Select just one piece or part at a time for revision in written form. Do not overwhelm students.

- Use the shorter writing processes such as quick-writes and sentence stems.

- Provide a reference booklet that contains frequently used vocabulary or spelling of the words involved with the unit learning goal and subject to be revised.

- Write out sentence starters and/or prompts for revision. Such starters may be "I understand there is a difference between obtuse and right angles and that difference is _____."

## Extending

There are many creative ways to extend knowledge using writing as a tool for revision:

- Suggest students create self-generated assessments as described earlier.

- Ask a small group of accelerated students to create multiple-choice assessment tasks for each other or the class.

## Instructional Technique 6

# REVISING KNOWLEDGE USING HOMEWORK REVISION

The final technique for revising knowledge involves reviewing and revisiting homework assignments. There are several important guidelines to keep in mind when assigning homework. You should give homework for the purpose of deepening knowledge about the content and/or practicing to achieve fluency in a process. A key prerequisite before assigning homework is giving students adequate time during class to deepen and practice under your watchful guidance. In the case of declarative knowledge, that means students will have multiple exposures to the content during class time. In the case of procedural knowledge, it means multiple opportunities to practice with teacher guidance and a gradual release of responsibility to the students. The bottom line is that students need to be prepared to work independently, without the need for the teacher (or parents) to be there to guide them.

As part of the homework discussion, the "flipped classroom" bears mentioning since it is gaining popularity. In the flipped classroom, the idea is to flip the common approach to instruction and homework. "With teacher-created videos and interactive lessons, instruction that used to occur in class is now accessed at home, in advance of class. Class becomes the place to work through problems, advance concepts, and engage in collaborative learning" (Tucker, 2012, p. 82). In the flipped classroom, "homework" is done in class, but the idea is still the same: responsibility is released from guided work/practice to independent work/practice with the ultimate goal of deepening knowledge and fluency in processes.

In this technique, students complete an assignment, the teacher gives feedback on the assignment, and students make revisions based on the feedback from the teacher. Students should be given time to make revisions after homework has been discussed and/or class activities that strive to deepen or practice knowledge.

One of the critical aspects of this technique is the feedback you give students. Your students' learning in the context of homework revision depends on the type of feedback you provide. Feedback achieves the greatest results when it is corrective, timely, criterion-referenced, and specific. "The best feedback appears to involve an explanation as to what is accurate and what is inaccurate in terms of student responses. In addition, asking students to keep working on a task until they succeed appears to enhance achievement" (Marzano, Pickering & Pollock, 2001, p. 96). To summarize, feedback should do each of the following:

- use specific vocabulary

- be directed to specific aspects of the student's work

- meet the needs of that student

- be clear

- include the next steps the student should take to improve

- include specific strategies the student can use to get there

## How to Effectively Implement Assignment Revision

Given the research discussed above, one effective method of implementation for individual student homework revision is as follows:

- When responding to homework, write effective feedback (see above) about what was accurate and what needs revision.

- If grades are necessary, record the grades in the grade book, but do not indicate the grades on the student homework.

- After returning the homework to the students, encourage them to revise and resubmit it to improve their grade. You may even want to give them time during class to make their revisions.

- Students revise homework based on the feedback you gave them.

- After the homework assignment has been revised and discussed, students should be encouraged to periodically revise their understanding of content by making new entries in their academic notebooks.

# Common Mistakes

The following is a list of common mistakes teachers might make as they are implementing revising knowledge using homework:

- The teacher tells students specifically how to revise the assignment by giving them the correct answer.

- The teacher fails to model revising homework/assignment strategies. As with the other strategies, students need some instruction on how to revise their homework as well as how to review the homework of their peers.

- The teacher moves too quickly through homework/assignment revision activities. Students need to be given time and guidance for the revision process.

- The teacher fails to monitor students for accurate understanding of information from the homework/assignment revision. Once students have revised their homework/assignments, teachers must review the revision work for accuracy and identify any remaining misunderstandings.

- The teacher tells students which questions were correct, then places students in groups so that they can simply copy the correct answer from their peers.

- The teacher focuses the revision on noncritical information or one specific aspect (e.g., grammar).

## Examples and Nonexamples of Revising Homework in the Classroom

The following are two examples (one elementary and one secondary) and their corresponding nonexamples for revising knowledge by revising homework assignments. As you read, think about experiences you have had in your classroom or observed in colleagues' classrooms. Consider the common mistakes, and note how the example teachers cleverly avoid them and the nonexample teachers miss the mark with their lack of understanding, planning, and foresight. Also, think about how a teacher might monitor for the desired result of revising knowledge.

### Elementary Example of Revising Homework/Assignments

The learning target for the elementary example is to *determine the unknown whole number in a multiplication or division equation relating three whole numbers. For example, determine the unknown number that makes the equation true in each of the equations 8 × ? = 48, 5 = _ ÷ 3, 6 × 6 = ?* (CCSS. Math.Content.3.OA.A.4). The third-grade teacher has been working toward this learning target for several days using manipulatives, word problems, and solving for unknown whole numbers. She concludes that her students are ready to work independently on these types of problems and assigns ten problems to be completed at home. Once she hands out the homework page, she explains how homework works in her class.

> Students, I want you to feel good about taking this assignment home and completing it all on your own. First, I'm going to model a problem just like the ones on your homework page. Watch, listen, and learn. *She works out the model problem.* Does anyone have a question about any of the steps I used? *Three hands go up, and the teacher answers the specific questions that each student has.* Now, I want each one of you to do the first problem on your own. As soon as you finish the problem, get with your assigned partner and compare your answers. If you have different answers, talk about how you solved the problem, and listen to your partner talk about solving the problem. See if you can agree on the correct answer.

At this point, the teacher divides the whiteboard into big squares. She puts the problem the class just solved into three of the squares and passes out the dry-erase markers. She asks individuals who disagreed with their partners to come up to the board to work the problem. Through this process, she and her students are able to correct mistakes. She carefully thanks those who made mistakes and thereby enabled others who might have made a mistake to revise their knowledge. When the teacher and students are satisfied that they have no more questions about the homework assignment, students gather their belongings and head home.

The next day, the teacher looks forward to correcting homework with the students. She uses the whiteboard method she introduced the day before and selects five of the homework problems to write in the squares. She selects five tongue depressors from a can on her desk, each one containing the name of a student, and assigns each student selected one of the problems to work on using the information from the homework assignment. Her goal during this exercise is to help students correct their mistakes, fill gaps in their procedural knowledge, or add important information they may have forgotten such as showing and labeling their work.

### Elementary Nonexample of Revising Homework

The elementary nonexample of revising homework is based on the same learning target. The teacher in this classroom is inconsistent in his application of routines for revising homework. On some days, he does not follow through on homework revision or even collect homework assignments. His students have followed his lead and often skip their homework, reducing their opportunities for both original learning and deepening knowledge by revising prior learning.

### Secondary Example of Revising Homework

The learning target for this classroom example is a long-range goal of middle school science: *construct explanations for the interactions of systems in cells and organisms and how organisms gather and use information from the environment* (MS-LSI-5). A middle school science teacher decides that rather than having students memorize the definitions of key terms in a particular unit as a weekly homework assignment, he will give them a more comprehensive homework task in the form of writing "show you know" sentences. Figure 6.1 displays a sample for the term *cell*.

At the beginning of the class period on the last day of the week, students are expected to turn in between three and five "show you know" sentences. The terms are assigned on Monday, and students have the week to work on them outside of class. They can use internet information, their textbook, and any resource materials in the classroom. Since constructing explanations is an important learning target, the teacher wants his students to have lots of practice writing using the language of science. He finds that the period in which he and the students go over their homework is particularly useful for revising knowledge. Here is how he and his students revise prior knowledge using their homework assignments. Before giving the assignment, the teacher modeled the completion of the template, thinking aloud about what information he knows and suggesting some places he might look if he needed more information. He demonstrates how to put other people's ideas into your own words rather than copying a definition word for word.

Class, I hope you're ready for checking your "show you know" sentences. I've divided the board at the front of the classroom into ten sections, and I'm drawing ten tongue depressors out of my can after I mix them all up. *The teacher pulls out ten tongue depressors, and the ten students whose names are called head to the board.*

People at the board, write your "show you know" sentence for the term *cell* in your assigned space. Remember to begin your sentence with a capital letter and end it with a period.

Don't get the idea that the rest of you narrowly escaped getting called upon. You are going to be the homework checkers today. Review all the sentences to see if you can find any mistakes that need to be corrected. Is there important information that should have been included? The big question to answer for each of these ten sentences is, did the authors show that they know something important about what a cell is?

In the process of checking over the sentences, the checkers notice that in some cases students wrote sentences that showed they do not know much about cells. The checkers ask those students to read aloud their answers to the first question: What is the meaning of the word *cell* in the context of biology? After checking and discussing their sentences, the teacher directs students to work with their partners to revise any of the information they included on their form and rewrite their "show you know" sentence to reflect any new information about cells they acquired that day.

**Figure 6.1: Sample "Show You Know" Sentence: *Cell***

| Directions: Write the term. Answer the questions about the term. Write a sentence that uses the word in a meaningful way by including words and phrases from the answers to your questions. | |
| --- | --- |
| Term: *cell* | |
| Question | Answer |
| What is the meaning of this word in the context of biology? | *A cell is the most important part of a living thing.* |
| What is the meaning of the word in another context? | *A cell can be a place to keep a prisoner, something that produces electricity, and also a mobile phone.* |
| When might this word occur in the context of biology? | *The word <u>cell</u> occurs very often since there are cells in all living things. So the word might be used in the study of photosynthesis, DNA, and how different traits are inherited.* |
| Why might this word occur in the context of biology? | *The word <u>cell</u> occurs as a central idea in the context of biology because it is the most important part of a living thing.* |
| "Show you know" sentence | *The human body contains about thirty-seven trillion cells, while some living things have just one cell.* |

*Secondary Nonexample of Revising Knowledge Using Homework*

The secondary nonexample classroom teacher is working toward the same learning target and has selected a set of terms for his students to process writing "show you know" sentences as a weekly homework assignment. He has not given much thought to how these assignments will be corrected and usually just collects students' papers as they exit the classroom. Later, as he looks over the papers, he realizes that many of his students have missed the point of the assignment and a large chunk of them did not even turn it in. He has not only missed an opportunity to help his students revise their prior learning on the spot, but also missed a chance to show his students that the assignment and his expectations were firm.

# Determining If Students Can Revise Knowledge Through Correcting Homework Assignments

Monitoring for the desired result of a specific technique is a critical part of using revising knowledge as a strategy. When you monitor for the desired result, students deepen their knowledge through making additions and deletions to previous knowledge, and you can truly assess how the homework/assignment you have given helps students achieve a deeper understanding of the content. We have included a few ways in the following list:

- Ask students to hand in the homework revisions, and read through them. Hand the homework back if additional revisions are necessary.

- Ask students to share their revisions with their partners or in groups, and listen and interject as you walk around the classroom.

- Have students turn in an exit slip completing statements such as "One new understanding I have is _____."

- Ask students to record any new understandings gained from the homework in their academic notebooks, and read the entries later.

- Ask students to record answers on whiteboards and discuss with their partners the accuracy and completeness of their responses.

Table 6.1 contains a student proficiency scale for revising homework. Use this to help you use the monitoring strategies outline above to determine the level of success each student is having with this technique.

**Table 6.1: Student Proficiency Scale for Revising Homework/Assignments**

| Emerging | Fundamental | Desired Result |
|---|---|---|
| Students revise homework/assignment mistakes inaccurately based on feedback.<br><br>Students may still be unable to decide what information is needed to correct misunderstandings. | Students identify understandings that were initially correct and/or incorrect.<br><br>Students can revise homework/assignments accurately and deepen understanding based on feedback to correct basic misunderstandings. | Students can successfully revise homework/assignments accurately and deepen understanding and make extensions and applications to the learning. They are able to state how those revisions clarified their understanding. |

# Scaffolding and Extending

The ways in which you scaffold or extend revising knowledge will depend on the specific needs of your students. Adapt your instruction using the following ways:

## Scaffolding

Here are some ways you can support students who are failing to complete and/or revise their homework accurately:

- Flip your classroom so all "homework" and revision is done in class. Those students who need support in the initial completion of homework will have the teacher there to guide them, and they will have something to work with when the time for revision begins.

- Scaffold the revision process by offering students multiple opportunities and ways to revise homework.

- Give precise feedback that clearly stipulates which information needs to be revised, without giving the correct answers.

- Give step-by-step directions on how to complete the revision process—what the student should do first, second, third, and so on.

- Have students partner or group to complete the revision. In those partnerships or groups, have a student with a solid understanding work with a struggling student.

- Work with a small group of students on the homework/assignment revisions while other students work on independent activities.

## Extending

A few methods for extending the revision lesson are as follows:

- Have students give a grade to their work after completing revisions and give a rationale for why they should receive that grade.

- Have students explain how the activity helped them deepen their knowledge.

- Have students help other students who need some assistance revising their homework.

# Conclusion

The goal of this guide is to enable teachers to become more effective in teaching content to their students. The goal of *revising prior learning* is to become skilled at teaching and modeling for students how to examine their own thinking and understanding about critical content to determine if they need to correct or amend what they know.

To determine if this goal has been met, you will need to gather information from your students, solicit feedback from your supervisor or colleagues, to find someone willing to embark on this learning journey with you. Engage in meaningful self-reflection on your use of the strategy. If you acquire nothing else from this book, let it be the *importance of monitoring*. The tipping point in your expertise and student achievement is *monitoring*. Implementing the strategy well is not enough. Your goal is the desired result: evidence that your students have developed a deeper understanding of the content by revising knowledge.

To be most effective, view implementation as a three-step process:

1.  Implement the strategy using your energy and creativity to adopt and adapt the various techniques in this guide.

2.  Monitor for the desired result. In other words, while you are implementing the technique, determine whether that technique is effective with the students.

3.  If, as a result of your monitoring, you realize that your instruction was not adequate for students to achieve the desired result, seek out ways to change and adapt.

Although you can certainly experience this guide and gain expertise independently, the process will be more beneficial if you read and work through its contents with colleagues.

# Reflection and Discussion Questions

Use the following reflection and discussion questions during a team meeting or even as food for thought prior to a meeting with your coach, mentor, or supervisor:

1. How has your instruction changed as a result of reading and implementing the instructional techniques found in this book?

2. What ways have you found to modify and enhance the instructional techniques found in this book to scaffold and enhance your instruction?

3. What was your biggest challenge, in terms of implementing this instructional strategy?

4. How would you describe the changes in your students' learning that have occurred as a result of implementing this instructional strategy?

5. What will you do to share what you have learned with colleagues at your grade level or in your department?

# RESOURCES

# Revision Template

| Used to Think | Now I Know |
| --- | --- |
| List of some initial understandings. | How those understandings in the left-hand column changed–additional knowledge or a misunderstanding that was corrected. |

# Interactive Notebook Example

| Notes | Revisions |
|---|---|
| Recording/representing critical information learned through teacher presentation, processing with others, elaborating activities, etc. | New understandings, insights, corrections of misunderstandings, etc. |

**Potential sentence starters for revision work:**

I learned that . . .

Something I have learned is . . .

I noticed that . . .

I changed my thinking about this concept when . . .

I still don't understand . . .

I used to think . . . but now I think . . .

# Academic Notebook Example

| Notes | Revisions |
|---|---|
| Recording/representing critical information learned through teacher presentation, processing with others, elaborating activities, etc. | New understandings, insights, corrections of misunderstandings, etc. |

**Potential sentence starters for revision work:**

I learned that . . .

Something I have learned is . . .

I noticed that . . .

I changed my thinking about this concept when . . .

I still don't understand . . .

I used to think . . . but now I think . . .

# Template for Peer Review of an Academic Notebook

| Read the Question and Review Your Classmate's Academic Notebook to Decide on an Answer | Write Your Answer in This Column |
|---|---|
| What methods did your classmate use to represent information that were especially clear, concise, and appropriate for the information being recorded (e.g., graphic organizers, flowcharts, concept maps, drawings, or pictographs)? | |
| What information did your classmate record that you did not record in your academic notebook? | |
| What do you think is the most important information recorded in your classmate's academic notebook? | |
| What is one thing that your classmate could improve on in recording knowledge in his academic notebooks? | |

# Consult/Compare/Explain Form

| Consult: Read My Classmate's Notebook | Compare: Revise My Notebook With New Information | Explain: Share Information With My Classmate to Identify Gaps or Incorrect Information |
|---|---|---|
| 1. | | |
| 2. | | |
| 3. | | |

# Agree/Disagree/Question Form

| What Does Our Group Agree About? | What Does Our Group Disagree About? | What Does Our Group Still Have Questions About? |
|---|---|---|
| 1. | | |
| 2. | | |
| 3. | | |

# Descriptive Pattern

| Meaning of the Term in My Own Words | My Visual Representation of the Term |
|---|---|
|  |  |
| After Reviewing My Prior Definition | After Reviewing My Previous Visual |
|  |  |
| After Reviewing My Prior Definition | After Reviewing My Previous Visual |
|  |  |
| My Final Definition of the Term | My Final Visual Representation |
|  |  |

# Snapshot Summary Template

| | |
|---|---|
| Snapshot Summary 1<br>Date _____ | Snapshot Summary 2<br>Date _____ |
| Snapshot Summary 3<br>Date _____ | Snapshot Summary 4<br>Date _____ |
| Snapshot Summary 5<br>Date _____ | Snapshot Summary 6<br>Date _____ |

# References

Ainsworth, L. (2010). *Rigorous curriculum design: How to create curricular units of study that align standards, instruction, and assessment.* Englewood, CO: Lead & Learn Press.

ASCD. (2012). *Resource guide: Grading and assessment.* Alexandria, VA: Author.

Bianconi, E., Piovesan, A., Facchin, F., Beraudi, A., Casadei, R., Frabetti, F., Vitale, L., Pelleri, M. C., Tassani, S., Piva, F., Perez-Amodio, S., Strippoli, P., & Canaider, S. A. *An estimation of the number of cells in the human body.* Retrieved March 14, 2014, from http://www.ncbi.nlm.nih.gov/pubmed/23829164

Brown, A. L., & Day, J. D. (1983). Macrorules for summarizing texts: The development of expertise. *Journal of Verbal Learning and Verbal Behavior, 22,* 1–14.

Common Core State Standards Initiative. (2010a). *Common Core State Standards for English language arts (ELA).* Washington, DC: Author. Retrieved September 9, 2014, from http://www.corestandards.org/ELA-Literacy/

Common Core State Standards Initiative. (2010b). *Common Core State Standards for mathematics.* Washington, DC: Author. Retrieved September 9, 2014, from http://www.corestandards.org/Math/

Dean, C. B., Hubbell, E. R., Pitler, H., & Stone, B. (2012). *Classroom instruction that works: Research-based strategies for increasing student achievement.* Alexandria, VA: ASCD.

DVPLearning. (2012, April 21). *Teach, do, review: An outstanding lesson.* Retrieved November 12, 2014, from http://evteachingandlearning.blogspot.co.uk/2012_04_01_archive.html

Education Development Center, Inc. (2014). *Video: Photosynthesis.* Retrieved from http://www.tv411.org/science

Fisher, D., & Frey, N. (2008). *Better learning through structured teaching: A framework for the gradual release of responsibility.* Alexandria, VA: ASCD.

Foorman, B. R., & Torgesen, J. (2001). Critical elements of classroom and small-group instruction promote reading success in all children. *Learning Disabilities Research and Practice, 16*(4).

Himmele, P., & Himmele, W. (2011). *Total participation techniques: Making every student an active learner.* Alexandria, VA: ASCD.

Marzano, R. J. (2003). *What works in schools.* Alexandria, VA: ASCD.

Marzano, R. J. (2007). *The art and science of teaching: A comprehensive framework for effective instruction.* Alexandria, VA: ASCD.

Marzano, R. J. (2009). The art and science of teaching: Helping students process information. *Educational Leadership, 67*(2), 86–87.

Marzano, R. J. (2010). *Formative assessment and standards based grading.* Bloomington, IN: Marzano Research Laboratory.

Marzano, R. J. (with T. Boogren, T. Heflebower, J. Kanold-McIntyre, & D. Pickering). (2012). *Becoming a reflective teacher.* Bloomington, IN: Marzano Research Laboratory.

Marzano, R. J., & Kendall, J. S. (2008). *Designing and assessing educational objectives: Applying the new taxonomy.* Thousand Oaks, CA: Corwin Press.

Marzano, R. J., & Pickering, D. J. (2005). *Building academic vocabulary: A teacher's manual.* Alexandria, VA: ASCD.

Marzano, R. J., Pickering, D. J., & Pollock, J. E. (2001). *Classroom instruction that works: Research-based strategies for increasing student achievement.* Alexandria, VA: ASCD.

Marzano, R. J., & Simms, J. A. (with T. Roy, T. Heflebower, & P. Warrick). (2013a). *Coaching classroom instruction.* Bloomington, IN: Marzano Research Laboratory.

Marzano, R. J., & Simms, J. A. (2013b). *Vocabulary for the Common Core.* Bloomington, IN: Marzano Research Laboratory.

Marzano, R. J., & Toth, M. (2013). *Teacher evaluation that makes a difference: A new model for teacher growth and student achievement.* Alexandria, VA: ASCD.

McEwan, E. K. (2004). *Seven strategies of highly effective readers: Using cognitive research to boost K–8 achievement.* Thousand Oaks, CA: Corwin Press.

McEwan, E. K. (2006). *How to survive and thrive in the first three weeks of school.* Thousand Oaks, CA: Corwin Press.

McEwan, E. K. (2007). *40 ways to support struggling readers in content classrooms, grades 6–12.* Thousand Oaks, CA: Corwin Press.

McEwan, E. K. (2009). *Teach them all to read: Catching the kids who fall through the cracks* (2nd ed.). Thousand Oaks, CA: Corwin Press.

McEwan-Adkins, E. K., & Burnett, A. J. (2012). *20 literacy strategies to meet the Common Core: Increasing rigor in middle and high school classrooms.* Bloomington, IN: Solution Tree Press.

Montis, K., & Pell, T. (2010). *The standard algorithm for dividing fractions.* Retrieved October 31, 2013 from http://web.mnstate.edu/peil/MDEV102/U3/S23/S235.html

Nagy, W. E., & Scott, J. A. (2000). Vocabulary processes. In M. L. Kamil, P. Mosenthal, P. D; Pearson, & R. Barr (Eds.) *Handbook of reading research* (Vol. 2, pp. 269–284). Mahwah, NJ: Erlbaum.

NGSS Lead States. (2013). *Next Generation Science Standards: For states, by states.* Washington, DC: National Academies Press.

Rutherford, P. (2008). *Instruction for all students* (2nd ed.). Alexandria, VA: Just ASK.

Schmoker, M. (2011). *Focus: Elevating the essentials to radically improve student learning.* Alexandria, VA: ASCD.

Therrien, W. J., Taylor, J. C., Hosp, J. L., Kaldenberg, E. R., & Gorsh, J. (2011). Science instruction for students with learning disabilities: A meta-analysis. *Learning Disabilities Research & Practice, 26*(4), 188–203.

Tomlinson, C. A. (2014, September). One to grow on/Releasing the will to learn. *Educational Leadership, 72*(1), 86–87.

Tucker, B. (2012). The flipped classroom: Online instruction at home frees class time for learning. *Education Next, Winter,* 82–83. Retrieved November 12, 2014, from http://educationnext.org

Wiggins, G., & McTighe, J. (2005). *Understanding by design.* Alexandria, VA: ASCD.

Willis, J. (2013, February 26). *Ask Dr. Judy webinar: Patterning to construct transferable concept memory.* Alexandria, VA: ASCD.

Witte, S. (2013). Preaching what we practice: A study of revision. *Journal of Curriculum and Instruction, 6*(2), 33–59.

Wormeli, R. (2006). *Fair isn't always equal: Assessing & grading in the differentiated classroom.* Portland, ME: Stenhouse.

# Index

# Notes

# Notes

# Notes

# Notes

# Notes

# MARZANO CENTER

## *Essentials for Achieving Rigor* SERIES

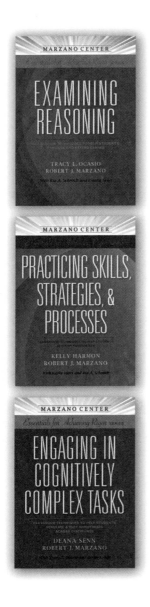

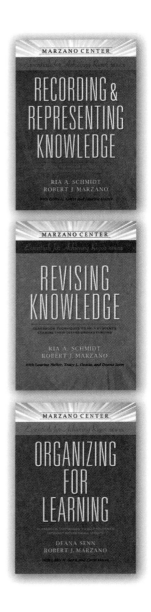

## Learning Sciences International
### LEARNING AND PERFORMANCE MANAGEMENT

Visit www.education-store.learningsciences.com or call 877-411-7114